FLYING TONIGHT

A SURVIVAL GUIDE TO AVIATION

PAUL HAWKINS

IAN ALLAN
Publishing

Foreword

It's traditional to start off by thanking everyone who has made this book possible. I'm no traditionalist. So first of all I want to mention my wife and kids, without whose constant interruptions this book would have been completed a long time ago. When I tell you that the hot news when I started writing it was the arrival of Lindbergh at Le Bourget, you'll get some idea of the enormity of the problem I've been up against. Because I'm such a rotten typist, and far too mean to employ a secretary, the real credit for this book should go to my computer and word-processing software, without whose help i woud have made a complite hasj of the wholr thing.

Incidentally, for those of you interested in such things, all the line drawings were also designed and printed by computer. During the production of this entire book, pen has not touched paper at all! Isn't technology marvellous? Heaven help me if we get a power-cut!

There are, though, some people who deserve a mention. It's either that or pay them, so here goes. The External Relations Department at Birmingham Airport allowed me access to the entire facility and Julie Cullen was a superb guide. My thanks also go to her for all the information provided. I was so impressed I nearly bought the Airport! Incidentally, Julie, I would like to apologise in public for having to body-search you when we came through customs, particularly since the contraband I suspected you of carrying turned out to be my umbrella! Look on the bright side, though — at least one of us enjoyed it!

Thanks also go to David Slack of Hogg Robinson Travel, who has booked me on so many flights (some of them to the right destination) and to the many airlines who provided information for this book and who have taken me safely all over the world for so many years. Incidentally, if you ever find my luggage, I would greatly appreciate its return. Who knows? Paisley shirts and flares might come back into fashion!

Finally, thanks go to Ian Allan for having the foresight to publish what will undoubtedly be a Number One International best-seller, and for providing so many photographs and helpful advice.

Paul Hawkins, 35,000 feet above somewhere very brown, 1994.

First published 1994

ISBN 0 7110 2243 7

Published by Ian Allan Publishing

an imprint of Ian Allan Ltd, Terminal House, Station Approach, Shepperton, Surrey TW17 8AS.
Printed by Ian Allan Printing Ltd, Coombelands House, Coombelands Lane, Addlestone, Weybridge, Surrey KT15 1HY.

Introduction

These days, I love flying. It wasn't always like that, however. I still remember my first-ever flight. It was a Dan-⎫ir Boeing 707 flying me off to the sun. And I was terrified. It wasn't just the flight itself, it was the whole thing — everything that goes with it. The check-in process, handing over my luggage, worries about missing my flight because I was in the wrong part of the airport. Then there was the take-off. What are all those whirrs and bumps? Why are the engines losing power when we need them most? Is it normal or are we going to crash? Landing was no better. The aircraft seemed to be all over the place. Getting out through a foreign airport was worse. All I could do was follow the masses and hope that they at least knew what they were doing.

Then I started to fly around the world on business as well as my annual pilgrimage to the sun. And things gradually got better. The process itself didn't change, of course. The whirrs, bumps and form-fillings were still there. But I was getting used to it. It didn't frighten me any more. And as I forgot all those problems, I began to get a lot more out of the flying experience. I suppose it's very much like driving a car. Do you remember your first driving lesson? I'll put money on the fact that you were so busy trying to remember how to steer and change gear at the same time, you didn't enjoy the scenery outside. You probably hadn't even got the foggiest idea of where you were! Then controlling the car itself became almost automatic. You were free to concentrate on the more pleasurable aspects of driving. That's exactly what this book is about. It will help you enjoy your flight. And enjoy it you should. After all it's cost you a lot of money.

I've now flown with more airlines to more destinations in more types of aircraft than I care to remember. I learned the ropes the hard way. And the novelty has never worn off. I seem to enjoy each flight more than the last. Whether it's non-stop to the Far East or the shuttle to Glasgow, you'll find me with a big grin on my face as soon as I get to the airport. I hope you are the same.

This book is in the form of an A-Z. It is written in such a way that you will be able to dip into it and quickly find the piece of salient information, in time to use it. If you suddenly get nervous because you've just heard an almighty thump coming from underneath the floor of the plane, I want to be able to tell you what it is before you have a heart attack! There is, inevitably, some repetition, because the subject items are closely interlinked. I've tried to keep this to an absolute minimum. Because subjects overlap, you will also find cross-references under each heading to help you 'home-in' on the subject you need.

So there it is. If you have bought this book in plenty of time, read it all before you leave for the airport. If you've only got this far and they're calling your flight for boarding, dip into it as and when you need it.

Most of all, enjoy your flight.

FLYING TONIGHT: A-Z

Aircraft (see also *Boeing, Concorde, Jet Engines*)

Most air-travellers have no idea which type of aircraft they are about to fly in. What's more, many do not know or care what they are sitting in or have just stepped out of. I always make it my business to find out the aircraft type at check-in. This isn't just because I am something of an enthusiast (although I suppose I am). If I know what kind of plane I am about to entrust my life to, then I can make sure I get the seat that is safest, is closest to the loo, has the best view of the film, is first to be served dinner or whatever else is important to me. If you, like many travellers, are no expert on aircraft, then simply state your requirements when you check-in.

My favourite long-haul aeroplane is definitely the 747, for a number of reasons. I must have travelled many hundreds of thousands of miles in the biggest civil airliner of them all, and there you have two of the reasons why I love it. Firstly, despite some problems with older planes, it is undoubtedly a very safe aircraft to fly in. The only problem I have encountered during all of those flying hours is an outboard leading-edge flap which failed to retract on a port wing shortly after take-off from Hong Kong. Although a nuisance, it was hardly life-threatening. Secondly, its size is a definite advantage to the passenger, particularly the nervous one. There is a feeling of space inside a 747 that you simply don't get with any other wide-bodied aircraft. Sitting in the centre seat block, it is sometimes difficult to believe that you are flying. The sheer size and weight of this aircraft means that the effects of turbulence are minimised and the ride is usually much smoother than travelling in a car. If you are the sort of person who likes to stretch their legs during a flight, you can move about in a 747 without walking around in tight circles! It's amazing to think that this 'monster of the skies' is about twice the length of the first flight by the Wright Brothers. Flying has come a long way in a very short time.

If you are flying a 747, you will be interested to know that they come in three basic types — the 200, the 300 and the 400. The 300-series is an

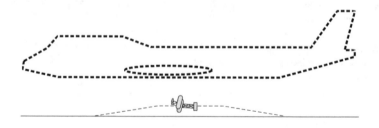

The Wright Brothers' first flight compared to a Boeing 747.

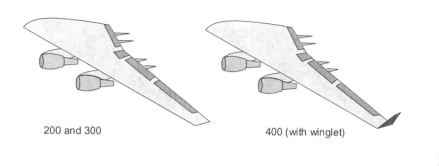

200 and 300   400 (with winglet)

KNOW YOUR 747

extended upper-deck version
of the 200. In other words, it
is bigger upstairs. The
400-series is the latest
offering from Mr Boeing
and has a longer range than
the 200 or 300. It also
contains the latest tech-
nology in avionics. You
can easily spot a 400 by the upturned
wingtips, known as winglets. Whichever type you are

"This is the Captain speaking.
Good news and bad news.
First, only two engines have failed.
Second, this is a twin-engined aircraft."

flying, you will be pleased to learn that they all have one thing in
common — four engines! Now, I know that jet engines have come a long way
in their development and I have seen all the statistics about the failure rates
and read all the articles that say how reliable they are. Frankly, in my opinion,
no matter how reliable they are I'd rather have four of them than two, which
seems to be the latest craze. There must be some doubts in the minds of the
powers-that-be about the safety aspects of twin-engined wide-bodied aircraft
such as the Boeing 757 and 767 and the like because a limit on flying time
from an airport has been imposed. I will always prefer as many engines as I
can get, regardless of what I read.

There are two other wide-bodied long-haul aircraft much favoured by
airlines. These are the McDonald-Douglas DC-10 and the Lockheed TriStar.
Both have three engines (which is slightly better than two), the third being
mounted on the tail section. The DC-10 has had somewhat of a chequered
history, but now seems to be a reliable aircraft after many design changes have
been incorporated. Certainly, it is a very nice plane to fly in. Several pilots
have told me that they prefer to fly a DC-10 than a 747. The TriStar is very

similar inside, and many passengers regularly mistake one aircraft for the other.

So much for the big boys. When it comes to short and medium-haul aircraft, there are so many different types that I couldn't possibly deal with them all. So let's just have a quick look at those that you are likely to encounter. The most common these days, and almost certainly the one that you will fly on holiday to Greece or Spain in, is the Boeing 737. Twin-engined and very comfortable, the 737 is a real little work-horse. I never cease to be amazed by what happens to the wings of these aircraft as they are landing. Try to sit in a window seat just behind the wing and watch. With the flaps fully extended and the air-brakes on, the wing virtually disappears!

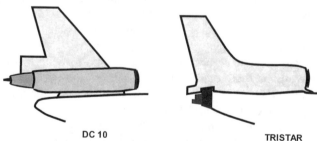

DC 10   **TRISTAR**

THE DC-10 AND L10-11 (TRISTAR) ARE OFTEN MISTAKEN
FOR EACH OTHER. THE TAILS ARE VERY DIFFERENT, HOWEVER.

The Boeing 737 is a common short and medium-haul jet.

The DC-9, often said to be the prettiest aircraft in the sky.

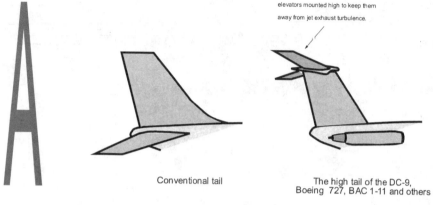

elevators mounted high to keep them
away from jet exhaust turbulence.

Conventional tail

The high tail of the DC-9,
Boeing 727, BAC 1-11 and others

TAIL TYPES

For slightly longer flights, you might find yourself in a Boeing 727. Mr Boeing has just about got this whole thing sewn up! Three engines, all at the back, the 727 is one long, thin aircraft. Sitting at the back and looking forward, you can almost convince yourself that you are in a cigar tube. Not really recommended for the heavy claustrophobics.

Much older, but still very much in use with many airlines throughout the world, is the DC-9. Considered by many to be the prettiest of all aircraft, the DC-9 was the most popular plane of the 1970s and early 1980s. It can be recognised by its two rear-mounted engines on the fuselage and its high tail. (The same basic design has been updated with the MD80.) The DC-9 has probably suffered more accidents than any other civil airliner. There have, however, been many reasons for disasters involving these aircraft and design problems are certainly in the minority. The elderly BAC 1-11 is a smaller aircraft which also has two rear-mounted engines and a high tail. It has been reported that the high tail design, which helps keep the elevators away from the turbulent engine exhaust, can result in these aircraft becoming deeply-stalled in unusual circumstances, from which recovery is very difficult. I hope never to be able to test this report!

The Twin Otter is used for short-haul shuttle flights.

All the aircraft described so far are jets. Indeed, the vast majority of all civil airliners flying today are jets but, on some very short routes, propeller and turbo-prop planes are used. In

Britain, the shuttles from the airports of the Midlands and North to Heathrow or Gatwick are usually of this type. Propeller aircraft are said to be the safest of all, but there are certainly some disconcerting things about flying in them. Firstly, they fly at much lower levels than the jets. In practice, in Britain, this means that most of the journey is likely to be spent flying through cloud, usually resulting in a fairly choppy ride. Secondly, they are very noisy machines to be in. The engine roar and whine can be deafening and you can actually feel the lower frequencies as vibrations in your head! At least the flights are short, so this does not have to be tolerated for too long. After a short hop on one of these, I always step on to the tarmac with a renewed admiration for the pioneers of civil flight who used to fly around the world in propeller-driven aircraft.

THIS IS THE FIRST AIRCRAFT I'VE SEEN WITH AN OUTSIDE TOILET!

Ork

Airlines (see also *Cabin Attendants, Business Class, Economy Class, First Class, Meals*)

I'd put money on the fact that you've turned to this section hoping to find me pontificating that 'the best airline is...' or 'whatever you do, don't fly with...'. Well, I'm not going to and that's that. The fact of the matter is that, even if I wanted to, I couldn't. Firstly, it is a matter of personal choice — one man's meat is

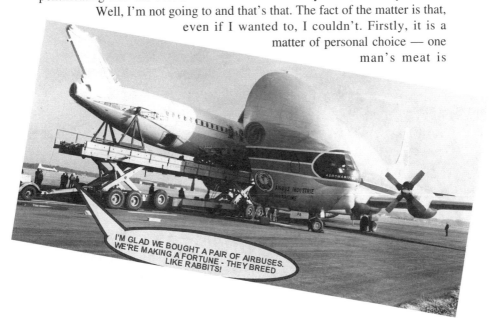

I'M GLAD WE BOUGHT A PAIR OF AIRBUSES. WE'RE MAKING A FORTUNE - THEY BREED LIKE RABBITS!

another man's poison and all that. Secondly and most importantly, I'd probably get sued!

By and large, any of the world's major airlines (and most of the minor ones) offer similar standards of service and comfort. There is a constant battle being waged between rival companies in this area since, if you think about it, it is one of the few ways that they have of attracting your custom. They all get you from A to B in the same type of aircraft, they are all subject to the same delays, winds and flight regulations. To find something unique to offer, each company must look beyond its main reason for

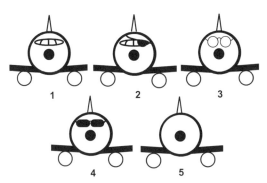

Airlines to fly (in order of preference)

existence, that of flying people around the world.

A large number of airlines use, at some stage in their advertising campaign, the concept of an 'image', usually based around their stewardesses (now officially called 'cabin attendants'). They all, if you believe what you read, have the most beautiful, mysterious and dedicated ladies whose only desire in life is to respond instantly with an engaging smile to your every whim. There is no doubt that the oriental airlines, particularly Cathay Pacific and Singapore, have a head start here. And they use it to the full.

Another tactic, and probably a more relevant one, is to point out the number of routes offered, how frequent the flights are and how many are non-stop. I have to admit that, in my case, this is a major consideration when choosing a carrier. If I can get a non-stop flight, and I can get it at the time of day I would like to fly, then I will almost always choose that airline. I hate stops *en route* even when I don't have to change planes. They waste time. Even the shortest of stops will add two hours to the journey when the additional descent and climb are taken into consideration. In addition, there's always the possibility that there will be delays in departing or that a boarding passenger, whose bags have been loaded, can't be found. That is why I welcome the introduction of new aircraft with ever-longer ranges. Non-stop flights are becoming more common all the time.

The choice of airline is normally very limited. The only exception to this rule is when you are flying a domestic route within the US. The choice in this case can often be absolutely bewildering. As a general rule, apart from travel to, from and within the States, the best airline to choose is one from your own country or the one to which you are travelling. So, for example, if you plan to fly to Australia from the UK, you should look first at Qantas and British Airways. This is not to say that there are no other options — indeed there are many — but they are likely to involve longer flying times and longer waits in airport lounges. The reason for this is quite simple. The route map for any one airline resembles the spokes of a wheel, radiating outwards from its main home-base airport, commonly called the 'hub' for obvious reasons. The Qantas hub is Sydney, that of British Airways is London, that of Lufthansa is Frankfurt and so on. Ideally, what you need is the shortest routeing and that would normally be along a 'spoke'. Any other choice will usually involve at least two spokes. For instance, using the previous example, you could choose to travel to Australia from the UK by flying Lufthansa or British Airways to Frankfurt and then Lufthansa or Qantas from Frankfurt to Sydney. Two spokes — see? To further complicate the issue, things can obviously be a little better if the two spokes are more or less in a straight line. At least the flight distance will not be increased by 'airline-hopping'. For instance, Singapore is more or less on a straight line drawn between London and Sydney. So routeing through Singapore and using Singapore Airlines would be relatively hassle free. Got the idea now?

Flying to the US opens a whole new world of possibilities. Again, the 'hub' system operates for the airlines of the US but the systems are so interlinked that lots of combinations are possible. When flying to the US from the UK you will usually find that the easiest option is to fly either British Airways, which operates services into most of the hub airports, or the US airline which uses your destination as its hub. For instance, if your destination is Atlanta, Georgia, the obvious choice would be Delta Airlines, since Atlanta is their hub. Many US airlines, however, have more than one hub. Very often, your final destination will not be one of the large hub airports. In that case, your choice of airline is much greater. If, for example, you want to go to Oklahoma City, then one possibility is Delta to Atlanta followed by Delta to Oklahoma.

The Multi-Hub system of Qantas based mainly on Sydney, Melbourne and Perth.

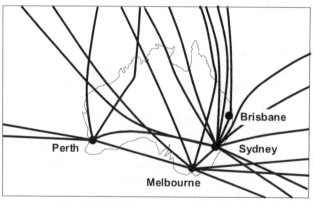

**The Multi-Hub system of Qantas,
based mainly on Sydney, Melbourne
and Perth**

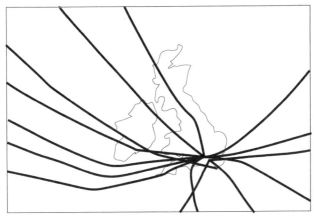

**The British Airways
Hub system, based on
London Heathrow and
London Gatwick**

The British Airways Hub system, based on London Heathrow and London Gatwick

Another is American Airlines to Dallas followed by American to Oklahoma. Yet another would be British Airways to Chicago, with a choice of carriers from Chicago to Oklahoma. And so it goes on.

Ease of travel and shortest flying times are certainly important considerations when choosing an airline. They are not, however, the only ones. Many other factors can be taken into consideration if they are important to you. Not all of them will be. Let's take a look, then, at some of the ways in which the airlines differ from each other.

Perhaps the most fundamental difference between the major international airlines is that of culture. Every carrier behaves more or less in the way that you would expect, given its country of origin. The Oriental airlines, for example, tend to have oriental cabin attendants, serve largely oriental food (although western food is usually available as an option), and have what can only be described as an oriental 'feel' to them. By the same token, an American airline is unmistakably American in its approach. If flying a Midwest airline, expect steak and eggs for breakfast and lots of whooping and hollering from the flight deck! The national carrier of Germany, Lufthansa, is known for its efficiency. Sleep when you are told to sleep and wake up when you are told to wake up! Qantas, the national airline of Australia, is unbelievably 'laid back' but still provides the service that its competitors achieve.

Airline food is the subject of almost as many jokes as the mother-in-law, but I really believe that it doesn't deserve such a bad reputation. Maybe I just have rotten taste in cuisine, but (dare I admit it?) I almost always enjoy in-flight meals. Having eaten on dozens and dozens of different airlines, and in

A

first, business and economy classes, I am nearly always pleasantly surprised. Of course, the portions are never enormous, but I have always given the airlines the benefit of the doubt. I assume that there is an expert nutritionist somewhere who has worked out exactly how much food a person needs to stave off the hunger pangs without feeling uncomfortably full. Well, it always works for me. The quality of the food is, in general, good. The carriers know very well that this is one of the main things that you are going to judge them on when making travel plans in the future. Virtually every airline now offers a free bar service in every class on medium and long-haul flights.

Safety is, for me, high up on the priority list. We all know that flying is, statistically, the safest form of travel. But that doesn't help much because there is something horribly final about a disaster in the sky. If you fall under a bus, there is a definite chance of survival. Not so if an aeroplane falls apart at 35,000 feet! I therefore avoid, as far as possible, airlines with a poor safety record or those with a very old fleet of aircraft. Remember that some 747s are now around 20 years old. I know a man that always asks the age of the aircraft before he boards. If the airline is evasive, or the answer is greater than 10, he simply gets a different flight. Many people refuse to fly in certain types of aircraft because they have a poor safety record. I have never taken things quite that far, but in general, all other things being equal, I prefer to fly in a relatively new 747 or a DC-10.

Comfort on board is important to many travellers. The number of seats in a cabin varies from airline to airline and obviously affects leg room. Charter flights often pack in far more seats than scheduled flights and journeys can be quite uncomfortable for a six-footer. A good tip if you are tall is to request a seat adjacent to an emergency exit, where there is always more room to stretch out. The spacing, or lack of it, between seats is the main difference between classes of cabin. Things are most cramped in economy class, are a little better in business class but are obviously best in first class, where there is enough room between seats to go dancing!

Probably the final main factor when choosing an airline is the cost of the ticket. This does not, however, vary all that much between comparable carriers. Airlines set up specifically to offer greatly reduced fares did so by reducing the level of service and by cramming as many people into a cabin as possible. Not surprisingly, they haven't withstood the test of time. Major cost differences only become important when comparing scheduled services with charter flights. There is no doubt that bargains can be had by taking spare seats on charter services, although there will normally be some restrictions on available flight times. Often, it will also be impossible to find out beforehand the type of aircraft or, indeed, the airline with whom you will be flying. Last-minute deals are usually made between carriers to maximise the use of their fleets.

So there we have it. Choose the airline with whom you feel most comfortable and which offers you the shortest flying time and most hassle-free trip. Flying is hard enough work without making it even more difficult for yourself!

Airports (see also *Delays, Departure Lounge, Immigration, Queues, Runway, Major UK Airports*)

Airports — the biggest problem with air travel. Wouldn't it be nice if a 747 pulled up outside your house like a taxi? Unfortunately, they just won't do it and it's always the same story — pathetic excuses like 'the wingspan's too wide to fit down your street'! So, as a result, we are all stuck with making our own way to the airport.

The first problem is getting there. With the latest check-in time firmly imprinted on your brain, there you are in a 20-mile queue on the M25, your blood pressure turning you the colour of a shepherd's sunset. I don't do it any more. My favourite method is to catch a shuttle flight from a local airport. The big advantage is that it puts you exactly where you need to be — right inside the international airport. There are, of course, always some disadvantages. Long waits for international flights are common. The shuttle flights themselves can be quite hair-raising on occasion; tiny aircraft that make deafening amounts of noise and spend their whole time flying through turbulent clouds. There's something very disconcerting about sitting right behind the pilot in these little aircraft and watching his every move. It makes him seem so, well, human to see him blowing his nose and scratching his back! But, on the whole, I'm sure that the advantages outweigh the disadvantages.

The other method of getting to the airport that I use occasionally is an airport taxi. Companies that operate taxis strictly for airport use can now be found in virtually any town or city. Amazingly, they are not much cheaper than shuttle flights and do not, of course, get away from the traffic problem. However, their drivers do this every day (poor sods!) and so they know all the short cuts. And if the worst happens, and you miss your flight, you've always got someone else to blame! This is a particularly useful piece of advice if you happen to be a junior executive and have to explain the whole thing to your boss.

The problems don't end when you get to the airport either — in fact they are only just beginning! First of all, you will need to know which airline you are flying with and where you are going. If all you

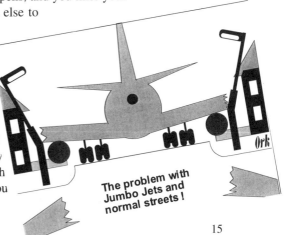

The problem with Jumbo Jets and normal streets!

**The Principal Shuttle Routes
To The London Airports**

have is your ticket, look in the space marked 'carrier'. There you will find a code such as 'BA' for British Airways or 'AA' for American Airlines, etc. A list of codes and the airlines they represent is included in this book. You need to know this because most major airports have several terminals which are often a long way apart. Heathrow, for instance, has a total of four terminals. If you are flying, say, British Airways on an intercontinental route, then the signs as you approach the airport will direct you to Terminal 4. If you are driving to the airport by car (ignoring my earlier advice), there is a separate car park for this terminal. Similarly, at Gatwick, there are different car parks for the South and (new) North Terminals. OK, so you have decided which terminal you need, have parked your car, making sure that you haven't left the ticket in it and have noted down exactly where your car is parked (although this will not necessarily help when you eventually try to find your car again!). You've caught the shuttle bus to the terminal building. Where now?

Airport designers seem to spend a great deal of their time looking for places to put vitally important counters so that the great flying public haven't got a hope in hell's

Finding your car in the carpark of a major
airport can be a problem if you haven't made
a note of exactly where you left it.

chance of finding them. Perhaps the greatest monument to their art is the siting of the check-in desk. Your next task is to locate yours, whilst laden down with all your baggage. At some airports, all the check-in desks for an airline are together. At others, business class check-ins and economy check-ins for the same flight might be at opposite ends of the building. To find your desk, you will need to know your airline, your flight number and your class of travel. First priority however has to be to find one of the infuriatingly elusive baggage trolleys!

After check-in, you will be armed with your boarding pass and can, if you wish, proceed through passport control to the departure lounge. Bear in mind, though, that there is no going back. So make sure you have said your good-byes and purchased various reading matter etc from the news stand before you go through. There will, of course, be some shops (including duty-free) in the departure lounge, but the choice of goods is often limited.

A view of the Gatwick Satellite terminal when it was nearing completion.

To get to the departure lounge, you will require your boarding pass and passport (if you are flying abroad). There will also be a security check where your hand-baggage will be X-rayed and you must walk through a metal-detector.

Once in the departure lounge, check the departure screens for details of your flight. Look for the boarding time and gate number. Now is your chance to purchase any duty-free items if you have time. You will need

17

Left: The Tour Operator desks are often in a different place to the scheduled flight desks. Right: If in doubt, the airport information desk should be your first port of call.

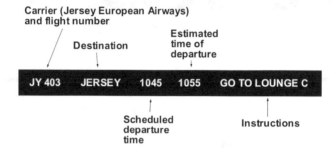

INFORMATION ON THE FLIGHT DEPARTURE BOARD

your boarding card.

When your flight is listed as 'Boarding', usually accompanied by flashing lights on the departure screen, go to the relevant departure gate. Have your boarding pass ready and board the aircraft.

Simple really isn't it?

Airshow (see also *In-Flight Entertainment*)

By 'airshow', I don't mean one of those exhibitions of flying where everyone pays vast amounts of money to watch aerobatic displays and a fly-by of Concorde. Incidentally, did you know that everyone inside Concorde is paying even larger sums of money for the privilege of a 'subsonic experience'? Concorde wins both ways. I don't know how they get away with it! No, by 'airshow', I mean the display found in many long-haul jets which gives you lots of information on where you are, where you have been and where you are (hopefully) going.

The display is projected on to the movie screen whenever a film is not being shown. It consists normally of several screens of information, with maps showing the progress of the aircraft, nearby places to look out for and other snippets of salient information such as the height of the plane, airspeed and

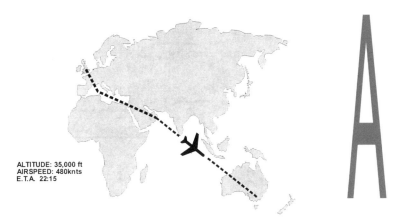

ALTITUDE: 35,000 ft
AIRSPEED: 480knts
E.T.A. 22:15

A TYPICAL AIRSHOW DISPLAY

windspeed. The airshow control system is linked into the aircraft's navigational equipment.

Several things have always puzzled me about these high-tech marvels. The first is that, if it is linked to the navigation system, how come that the airshow often tells you that you have arrived when a quick low-tech look out of the window tells you that you are still at 20,000 feet? I just hope that the navigation system is a little more accurate than the airshow! Secondly, the 'places of interest' shown along the route are the most obscure names in the world. You will see names such as 'Zog' and 'Blasscanovitch'! Even when approaching Gatwick, you will not see it named but will see 'Chartwell'. I can only presume that they are the names of navigation beacons or something along those lines. These airshow displays also manage to make the journey seem longer than it is. It's the same principle as 'a watched kettle never boils'. To see your aircraft creep like a geriatric snail across the map is a painful experience. Try as you might, you can't help but look at it every few minutes to see how far you have moved, only to discover you haven't!

So my advice is this. If you've never seen one of these marvels of electronic wizardry before, have a look shortly after take-off, be impressed and then don't look at it again — ever!

Air-Sickness (see also *Alcohol, Dutch Roll,*
Fear of Flying, Jet-Lag, Sleeping, Turbulence, Weather)

I have to admit that air-sickness is not something I have ever suffered from. The same goes for any form of motion-sickness, although a very stormy North Sea ferry crossing a few years ago brought me closer to it than I have ever been before or since! I can only assume that the same must go for the vast majority of my fellow passengers, since I have never seen anyone being sick

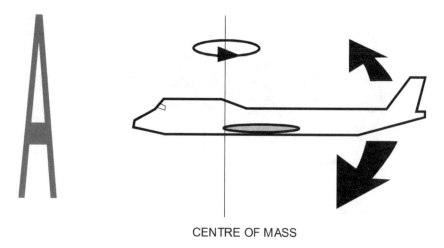

CENTRE OF MASS

The sideways movement or yawing is much more noticable at the rear of the aircraft, since it is furthest from the centre of mass of the plane.

on an aircraft. This is hardly surprising. The smooth ride of modern jets is hardly likely to upset even the most delicate digestive system. That said, very nervous passengers might be affected, particularly in areas of turbulence, and airlines continue to supply the old faithful paper bag in every seat pocket. I've often wondered why, in this day and age, can't they be plastic?

If you are one of the unlucky minority who begin to feel nauseous during a flight, there are a couple of things you can do. Relax yourself as much as you can and take slow, deep and deliberate breaths. Many people find that sipping iced water is a big help. The cabin attendants often have their own remedies, so don't be afraid to ask them. Look out of the window and concentrate on whatever you can see that is fixed, such as clouds or some particular ground feature.

As with most things in life, prevention is better than cure. If you are nervous about your forthcoming flight, then don't eat an enormous meal before boarding, and stick to light snacks during the flight. Sandwiches are always available. It is always tempting to drink alcohol, especially when you are nervous, but you should avoid it like the plague. Try not to smoke and sit in a non-smoking cabin to avoid the fumes. Choose your seat with care. Avoid sitting right at the back of a large aircraft. The tail section, because it is a long way from the centre of gravity, tends to accentuate any buffeting of the plane. I can still remember my first trip in the last seat row of a 747. During our initial climb, apart from the usual up and down movement, I was being thrown from side to side in my seat in a most violent manner. The huge tail tends to act as a 'weathercock', lining up with the wind as it gusts in slightly different directions. You simply don't notice the effect when sitting further forward.

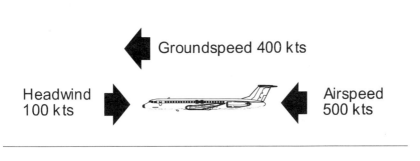

The difference between airspeed and groundspeed.

Airspeed (see also *Flaps, Groundspeed, Jet Engines, Landings, Stalls*)

This is a very important item. It is airspeed that keeps you in the air. Forget the champagne — without airspeed you've had it. So what is it? Well, I don't suppose it will get me a place on 'Mastermind' to say that it is the speed of the aircraft in the air, but that's exactly what it is. This must not be confused with groundspeed. The latter is, of course, the speed over the ground and is what gets you to your destination. However, the air is rarely still and this greatly influences airspeed. For instance, if your groundspeed is 400 kts and you have a head wind of 100 kts, then your airspeed is 400+100=500 kts. If, on the other hand, you have a tail wind of 100 kts, your airspeed will be 400-100=300 kts.

The lift generated by the wings is dependent on the wing moving through the air or the airspeed. No airspeed — no lift. You will quickly spot, therefore, that if your groundspeed is, say, 200 kts and you have a tail wind of 200 kts, then you are in serious trouble! This, you will be grateful to learn, doesn't happen. The engines are there to provide airspeed by propelling the aircraft

Aircraft will always land into the wind to reduce groundspeed whilst maintaining airspeed. They will take-off into the wind to build up airspeed as quickly as possible.

21

forward through the air. So, in practice, a tail wind is a bonus because it increases your groundspeed. So you reach your destination that bit quicker.

The only time when a tail wind can be a problem is when taking off or landing. I'm sure that you have noticed that aircraft take off or land in different directions on different days. You may also have noticed that the direction of take-off and landing is the same. This is because aircraft should always, as far as possible, take off and land into the wind. During the roll down the runway, the flow of air over the wings must reach a minimum speed before the plane can fly. A head wind is a help because it allows a plane to reach its minimum airspeed when travelling relatively slowly. If, on the other hand, you have a strong tail wind, then the plane must charge down the runway like a bat out of hell to reach its take-off speed! A similar sort of situation exists when landing. Because the aircraft must maintain a reasonable airspeed on its final approach, if there is a tail wind the groundspeed on touchdown can be quite frightening!

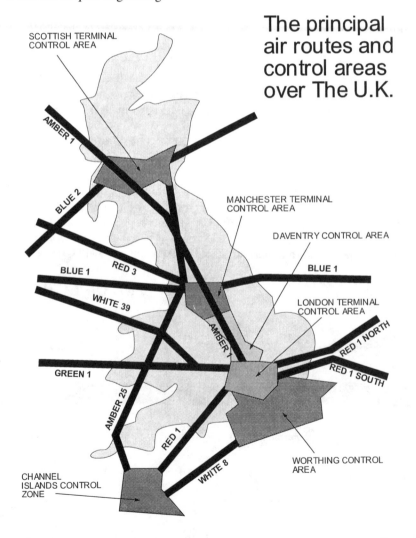

The principal air routes and control areas over The U.K.

SCOTTISH TERMINAL CONTROL AREA

AMBER 1

BLUE 2

BLUE 1

RED 3

WHITE 39

MANCHESTER TERMINAL CONTROL AREA

DAVENTRY CONTROL AREA

BLUE 1

AMBER 1

LONDON TERMINAL CONTROL AREA

RED 1 NORTH

RED 1 SOUTH

GREEN 1

AMBER 25

RED 1

WORTHING CONTROL AREA

CHANNEL ISLANDS CONTROL ZONE

WHITE 8

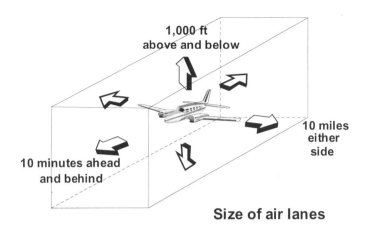

Size of air lanes

A typical ATC radar screen, showing squawk ident information (call sign and altitude) and direction..

The screen is updated every few seconds.

Air Traffic Control (see also *Delays, Disasters, Flight Level, Radar, Radio*)

Everyone has heard of air traffic control. Unfortunately, it is one of those organisations that only seem to get a bad press — never good. Who wants to read or hear about how many aircraft were successfully routed through the skies of the world today? We only hear of these backroom boys and girls when a near-miss occurs or the computer at West Drayton breaks down for the third time this week. The fact is that these organisations throughout the world do a remarkably good job separating civil airliners, military traffic and private pilots every hour of every day.

The movement of a passenger aircraft is controlled from the moment it gets clearance to start its engines, to the moment it pulls up to the jetway at its destination and shuts its engines off. No other form of transport is so closely monitored by so many skilled people and with such high-technology equipment.

All aircraft are required to fly through specific corridors, 10 miles wide. They will be separated vertically by at least 1,000ft and horizontally by at

A least five miles or 10 minutes flying time. There are also specific terminal control zones surrounding the major airports. All of this is monitored by the Air Traffic Controllers, most of whom sit in darkened rooms, often miles from airports, spending all their time watching radar screens with their computerised graphics. But how does it all work?

A flight starts under the direction of the ground movement controller who gives the Captain clearance to start his engines, push back and taxi to the runway. He will use ground radar to ensure that all the aircraft under his control get to where they want to be without getting too close to each other.

The Tower gives the aircraft its initial climb and vector instructions, together with its 'squawk ident' code. When activated, this gives the plane's

What looks like the new Control Tower at Birmingham Airport is, in fact, apron control. The old tower is still used for air traffic control.

call-sign and height alongside its radar blip. Approach Control guides the aircraft through its climb, ensuring that it stays away from other ascending and descending aircraft.

Control is then taken by the Air Traffic Control Centre. The Centre monitors its progress and the crew report position and height regularly.

During the flight, control will be passed to different control centres, until nearing the destination it will first be picked up on radar, together with its squawk information. Eventually, it will come within VHF radio range and will then be in voice communication with the approach controller, who will give descent instructions.

Finally, after landing, it is back under the control of a ground movement controller who looks after the aircraft until it is safely parked at its gate with the engines switched off.

Alcohol (see also *Colds and Flu, Drinking, Fear of Flying, Meals, Sleeping*)

Now here's an emotive subject! The easiest thing to say under this heading is — Don't! But, luckily, I am a realist. Virtually everyone likes a drink on an aeroplane. I am no exception. Apart from any other reason, it helps to pass the time. The problem is that, on most medium and long-haul flights, the drinks are free and time is plentiful. This, of course, makes it very difficult to say no. I can, as they say, resist everything but temptation!

In fact, a little alcohol will not cause any great harm. It adds to the enjoyment of your meal, helps you relax and makes sleeping easier. Too much alcohol, however, will add to the problems of flying. People tend to dehydrate very quickly in-flight and alcohol makes this worse. Hangovers can be dreadful. If you find yourself drinking too much, at least drink plenty of water as well to help overcome this effect. Alcohol also, in my case (and with most people) adds to the problem of jet-lag. You are going to feel bloody awful at the end of a long flight in any case, so the best way to attack this is to ensure that you are in reasonable physical shape. A spinning head and a mouth that feels like the bottom of a ferret's cage is the last thing you need when queuing for immigration control.

The advice, then, is by all means have a drink, but don't get stupid with the liqueurs or you'll regret it. Here endeth the lesson. If you choose to ignore me and end up wishing for a quick, painless end to it all in the immigration queue, and someone taps you on the shoulder and says 'It serves you right' — don't bother to look round. It will be me.

Altitude (see also *Air Traffic Control, Automatic Pilot, Jet Engines, Landings, Sound Barrier, Vapour Trails, Weather*)

After ascent, at Top Of Climb, most flights will stay at more or less the same altitude until they begin the descent towards the destination airport. This is normally referred to as the Flight Level. A flight level of 350 is, for instance, 35,000ft. This altitude is, incidentally, the one most favoured by long-haul

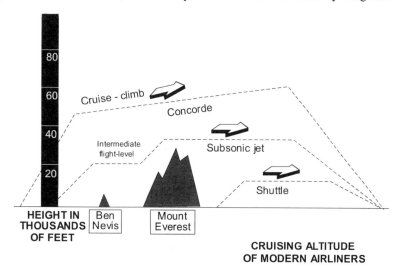

CRUISING ALTITUDE
OF MODERN AIRLINERS

pilots since turbulence is at a minimum and the jet engines are at their most efficient at this height. Our air lanes are, however, becoming increasingly congested and so air traffic control often has to allocate a different flight level for at least part of the flight. Occasionally, the pilot himself will request a different flight level to avoid bad weather such as very strong head winds.

Propeller-driven aircraft will fly lower. Most of their routes are so short that they simply wouldn't have the time to climb to 35,000ft, even if they wanted to do so. The air shuttles often climb to 10,000-12,000ft.

The other exception to the rule is my own favourite aircraft (and virtually everyone else's) — Concorde. The first lady of the sky has the civil airliner heavens to herself at around 50,000-55,000ft. The sky at this altitude is definitely darker and there is a marvellous feeling of being close to space itself. Some people even report that the curvature of the Earth is visible.

Automatic Pilot (see also *Airshow, Fly-by-Wire, Instrument Landings, Navigation*)

Watching the film 'Airplane' has poisoned my mind. I can't read the words 'automatic pilot' without thinking of that self-inflating man that bobs up from the Captain's seat and takes control of the joystick!

In real life, of course, as is the case with most things, it's not nearly as attractive as that. The automatic pilot (which used to be called 'George' for some reason) is merely a computer, or three computers, to be precise. The first takes on the business of flying the aircraft. The second one watches exactly what the first one is doing. The third makes the tea! No, it's actually a spare, in case one of the first two decide to have a mental breakdown in mid-flight.

**A modern airliner has 3 Autopilots
for failsafe operation.**

I'm sure they route our bags
all over the world as a joke!

The high-tech baggage handling system in operation. Guess which case will fall off first!

The automatic pilot does just about everything these days. It will be engaged shortly after take-off and will climb the plane to its initial cruising height on the correct course, make the correct turns at the right places, in conjunction with the Inertial Navigation System, and constantly monitor the performance of the aircraft, alerting the crew to any problems if necessary. The crew make sure that everything is OK, but provided the correct information has been fed into the computer in the first place, it is virtually foolproof.

Most destination airports have the necessary equipment for auto-landings, in which case the automatic pilot will bring the aircraft down on to the tarmac without the crew touching anything. Once down, the computer is disengaged and the aircraft is taxied to the apron manually.

As you have probably gathered by now, there are long periods during the flight when the crew have little to do. This situation has brought about its own set of problems. Inactive minds tend to be less alert, and anything less than a fully alert mind is unacceptable if an emergency suddenly presents itself. Even when this is taken into consideration, though, the thing that scares me most is the prospect that very soon the Captain and First Officer will be replaced by yet another blasted computer!

Baggage (see also *Baggage Allowance, Bombs, Carousel, Check-In, Dangerous Articles, Duty-Free, Hand-Baggage, Lost Property*)

Have you ever been to Bombay? No, but my baggage has! So goes the old joke. Is there any truth in this? Would an airline, whom you have entrusted with your baggage (not to mention your life) be careless enough to lose it? Read on for the whole, horrible truth!

I hate to admit it, but in the whole of my flying career, my luggage has only been lost once — and even then it arrived less than 12 hours late!

To avoid embarrassment, always make sure that your cases are securely locked!

FLYING TONIGHT: A-Z

Maybe I've just been lucky. It probably helps that I only ever travel with one piece of checked-in baggage. If it doesn't fit in that one case, I don't take it! Certainly, I've heard plenty of horror stories from fellow passengers that bags regularly go missing for days or weeks at a time, and sometimes

DON'T BE AFRAID TO MAKE YOUR BAGS STAND OUT IN A CROWD !

never turn up again at all. Frankly, I think that a lot of these stories are greatly exaggerated and are told only because it's what people want to hear. These days, cases are computer-traced and the worse that can happen under normal circumstances is that your luggage arrives on the next flight. The airlines will then usually deliver your cases directly to you at your home or wherever you are staying. As long as you report your cases missing as soon as possible to the baggage handlers, you should not have too many problems.

So what about your cases themselves? Well, there are different opinions on the best type to have. The only really useful rule is this: keep the number of cases to an absolute minimum. Many people seem to prefer hard cases. They are obviously less vulnerable to damage, as are their contents. The main advantage of soft cases, however, is that they are often first off the plane because they tend to be loaded last, on the top of the pile. Don't choose cases that are too big. The weight of a full case might seem OK when you lift it for a few seconds in your bedroom, but when you are trying to cross a busy road to get into the terminal after walking from the car park, I can guarantee that it will seem a whole lot heavier!

Do make sure that your luggage is distinctive and secure. You need to be

KNOW YOUR BAGGAGE TAG
1. THE FILTHY RICH (OR UPGRADE EXPERT)

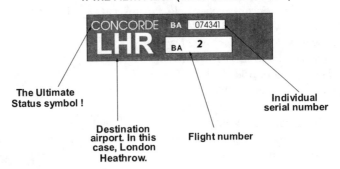

The Ultimate Status symbol !

Destination airport. In this case, London Heathrow.

Flight number

Individual serial number

able to pick it out in a crowd of similar cases when it comes round on the dreaded carousel. And you want to be sure that, despite the attentions of the handlers, it is closed and everything is inside it when it appears. I've seen many a fine woman faint when her case appears, burst open and with a frilly pink G-string casually hanging half out of it! The best and cheapest way to avoid both problems is to buy one or two of those gaudily coloured straps for each case. You can usually buy them in the airport shops.

Make sure that your name, flight number, destination airport and final address are clearly marked on each item of luggage. Don't forget, when checking your cases in, to offer up the air-traveller's blessing 'May your case be with you'!

Baggage Allowance (see also *Baggage*)

Obviously, the space inside an aircraft is limited. If it is to get off the ground, so is its weight. It is therefore necessary to impose upper restrictions on the size and weight of luggage you can take with you.

Your baggage allowance depends to a certain extent on the type of flight and your class of travel. Generally, though, in terms of carry-on luggage, you will be allowed one piece weighing not more than 5kg and of a size that will fit in either the overhead lockers or under the seat in front of you. Ladies come off slightly better, because they are also allowed a handbag. I don't know how they get away with some of the handbags I've seen being taken into the cabin. I swear they could get the kids inside! You will also be allowed a camera or similar small item and your bag of duty-free goodies.

Checked-in luggage allowance is normally two pieces, not exceeding 20kg in weight. If travelling First Class, the weight limit is increased to 30kg. On charter flights, the limit of 20kg normally applies.

If you haven't got a set of scales, the rule of thumb is that if you can just lift your case off the ground with one hand, you will be OK. If it takes two hands, you will probably be OK. If you can't lift it, either you are a weakling or you're going to pay an excess baggage fee. No liability for any of the above is accepted if your name is Geoff Capes.

On the subject of excess baggage fees, a little moan. It seems to me that it's a bit of a con. Whilst I accept that if the aircraft is heavier, it's going to burn more fuel and so cost the airline more, I can't accept that you should automatically have to pay every time your bags are overweight. I normally travel very light. If my case weighs more than 5kg, I'm in the process of emigrating. So why can't some other passenger use my spare 15kg without having to pay for it? After all, the airline has already budgeted for it. How would this work, you will be asking, if you have even the slightest interest in the subject. Allow me to enlighten you. During check-in, the desk would keep a cumulative total of the weight of bags checked-in so far, compared to the total if everyone was

JUST HAND THIS IN AT THE DESK, SIR, AND I'M SURE THAT THEY'LL FIND YOUR LUGGAGE EVENTUALLY!

smack on their allowance.

So if 20 people had already checked-in and the total baggage weight was 320kg, the figure would read 320-400, or -80. Then if someone came along with 5kg of excess, it would be allowed free and the figure would change to -75. 'That's not fair' I hear you screaming. The first person can never carry free excess baggage. And if you are following several people in the queue with loaded trolleys, you haven't got much chance either. I agree that's true, but surely it's better than everyone having to pay regardless. To get round it, we'll all just have to be a bit more canny. If you're carrying the European Luggage Mountain, get in the queue behind someone like me, who only has a toothbrush sticking out of his jacket pocket. Jostling for position would not be allowed. It might even develop better queuing manners. Instead of the usual push for the front, the one-man removal companies would be hanging back, saying to the likes of me 'After you, sir'!

AIRLINE BRITISH AIRWAYS		SPECIAL INFORMATION CONCORDE	BRITISH AIRWAYS
			CONCORDE
FLIGHT DATE DEST CLASS BA0002 22APR LHR R		SERVICE INFORMATION VIP	
NAME HAWKINS P	SEAT NR 10A	10A	
			Boarding pass

The Author's Concorde Boarding Card, Vintage 1989.

Boarding Card (see also *Check-In, Duty-Free, Gate*s)

When you check-in for your flight, you will be given a boarding card which states the flight number, destination, date, your name, class of travel and your seat assignment. When you first get it, please check it well to make sure that all the details are correct. The boarding card is printed out by computer and I have known several errors that have crept into the process. In the past, I have been given boarding cards with other people's names on them, cards for the wrong flight and cards with the wrong seat assignment. If all the details are correct, my next piece of advice is — don't lose it ! Your boarding card is the most important piece of paper that you have, together with your passport. Without it you will not be allowed to board your plane. You will also need to show your boarding card to get into the departure lounge and to buy duty-free items. Make sure that you hang on to your boarding card even after you are sitting in your seat — it's not unknown for seats to be double-booked and when someone else tries to sit on your lap, it's nice to have proof that you were assigned the seat that you are sitting in. So I'll say it again. Do not lose your boarding card.

Boeing (see also *Aircraft, Jumbo Jet*)

If you have travelled in a jet aircraft, it's an odds-on bet you've been in a Boeing. Whether you've been on a short, medium or long-haul flight, Mr Boeing has a plane for you — and plenty of them! The modern Boeings started with the 707; a four-engined medium-haul aircraft that revolutionised sky-travel. 707s have been around for a long time now, but you may still find them operating occasionally as charter aircraft, and very good they are too. In the late 1960s, Boeing did it again with the development of the first wide-bodied civil jet, the 747. The 747, in its latest form — the 400-series — is still going strong and is still the only civil airliner in the world with an 'upstairs'. After the 747, Boeing decided to get into the short and medium-haul market and came up with the 737, a twin-engined plane that has proved very popular with the world's airlines. The next offering from Seattle was the medium-range 727, a three-engined machine, very popular with airlines in the US for intermediate distance domestic routes. The 1980s saw the development of medium and long-haul 'big twins' — large aircraft using two engines and advanced flight-control systems. Again, Boeing is well represented with the 757 and 767.

The only serious rivals to Mr Boeing's dominance in this field are McDonnell-Douglas with the famous DC-9 medium-range and DC-10 long-range aircraft, and now the MD-80, an updated version of the DC-9; and Lockheed, which is known these days only for the TriStar, a long-range aircraft using three engines in a similar configuration to the DC-10. Newcomers to the scene are Airbus Industries, a joint European consortium, with its Airbus series of medium and long-range aircraft.

With the 707, 727, 737, 747, 757 and 767, wherever you want to fly, Boeing has got the aircraft for you! The only thing that continues to mystify

people is 'what happened to the 717?' Yes, it did exist, but it wasn't a passenger jet. When Boeing first began the development of a jet airliner, the outcomes of the programme were the 707 and the KC-135 military jet, known within Boeing as the 717. The aircraft had several variants, including one for refuelling bombers (the Strato Tanker) and another 'special-purpose' type. Almost certainly, the 'special purpose' was aerial reconnaissance and other secret activities during the Cold War. It is thought that one of these aircraft was the real target when the USSR shot down Korean Airlines' flight 007 in 1983. Production ended in 1986, but many are still flying.

What's going to be next from Seattle? Well, Boeing is already well-advanced with the development of the 777. It will be a twin-engined wide-bodied jet, capable of extended range and promising new levels of operational economy for the world's airlines. The avionics will, of course, be state-of-the-art, with computer control and fly-by-wire control systems. It will be the largest twin-engined jet in the skies and many airlines are already showing signs of preferring it over its main rival, the four-engined Airbus A340. The people mover of the 20th century has been the 747. We must wait to see which aircraft dominates the skies in the year 2000 and beyond.

Bombs (see also *Disasters*)

Now I wonder how many would-be international terrorists have bought a copy of this book and have flipped straight to this section, hoping for handy tips on how to make one? Sorry, you've just bought the wrong book.

The fact of the matter is, and I hate to have to admit this, my biggest fear of flying (apart from being locked in the toilet with Erica Jong) comes from wondering whether there is a bomb on board. This is a terrible reflection on the age in which we live, and I am sure that I'm not alone in being afraid. Press reports seem to suggest that most of these devices (and thank God there aren't many of them) are altitude triggered. I am always, therefore, relieved when we reach cruising altitude.

Airport security has, of course, been tightened considerably in recent years although I continue to wonder just how difficult it is to get an explosive device aboard, even these days, if one is determined enough. Plastic explosives, we are told, do not show up in X-rays and can only be detected by extremely expensive electronic gadgetry which is in very short supply. I don't like to have to say it, but I still believe some airports are wide-open targets for well organised terrorist attacks.

I warmly welcome any extra security measures that can be taken to minimise the risks of bombs being loaded on to aircraft, even if the measures result in a considerable increase in delays at airports and higher fares. I know full well that there would be a lot of moaning from some people because of missed business appointments and the like, but, at the end of the day, you simply can't put a price on a human life. I also believe that it would be in the airlines' best interests to maximise security. Look at what happened to Pan Am after the Lockerbie disaster. The same thing would happen to any other airline that was at the centre of a similar tragedy. So please, airport authorities, airlines and anyone else who is reading this, do whatever is necessary to eliminate this obscene threat as quickly as possible.

On the brighter side, it's worth remembering that the incidence of explosives on aircraft is absolutely minute. I've no idea what the figures are, but a statistician would probably tell me that I'm more likely to be killed by a one-legged Martian on my way to the airport than by a terrorist bomb. So please don't get the risk out of proportion and don't let it ruin your flight.

Bumping (see also *Check-In, Latest Check-In Time, Tickets*)

Sounds painful, doesn't it? When I were a lad, we used to get bumped in the playground by those enormous 12-year-old six-footers that are a compulsory part of the British educational system. From what I can remember, it consisted of being hoisted up by hands and feet and then dropped on to the tarmac playground in a thinly-disguised attempt to fracture your spine. Quaint eh? Since my own boys have never come home doing Quasimodo impersonations, I can only assume that the habit has died out. They probably mug each other now instead.

Anyway, this has got nothing to do with the sort of bumping I mean. I am talking about not being allowed to board your aircraft, even though you have a confirmed reservation. Airlines often overbook, in an attempt to compensate for those people that buy tickets and then don't check-in for the flight (the 'no-shows'). If tickets were non-transferable and non-refundable, there would be no problem. No one would buy a ticket and not use it. But the situation is that an unused ticket can be transferred to any other flight and so many people, especially business men, decide to take later flights without telling anyone. So the airlines try to get round this by selling more tickets than there are seats.

Sometimes, however, everyone shows up and someone is going to be disappointed.

It isn't actually as bad as it sounds. If, on a particular occasion, everyone shows up, then volunteers are called for who are willing to be put on another flight, or 'bumped', as it is known. Passengers who agree to this will always be compensated in some way, either

That's the last time I volunteer for bumping!

Ork

B

financially or by an upgrade on the next flight. In the rare cases that there aren't enough volunteers, then passengers will be forcibly 'bumped', but will still receive compensation.

I quite enjoy the opportunity to volunteer for 'bumping'. It has provided me with many first class and Concorde flights over the years, together with many nights in five-star hotels, all free of charge. It used to be a cottage industry at Kennedy Airport in New York. You bought a business class ticket on the Friday evening Jumbo to Heathrow and then checked-in as early as you could. The first few had always got a good chance of volunteering to give up their seat on the flight in exchange for an overnight stay in an airport hotel and a flight back on the Saturday Concorde. If you're not in a desperate hurry to get there, take my advice. Try a bump!

Business Class (see also *Economy Class, First Class*)

(Also known as Club World, Marco Polo Class, Royal Ambassador Class and dozens of similar silly names, depending on which airline you are flying with.)

The only experience that most people who fly will have had of business class is when walking through it to get to the cheap seats at the back! When you are flying business class, the airline usually allows you to board first so you are already in your seat, sipping from your glass of champagne, when the hordes travelling in economy class (or 'main cabin' as it is tastefully now called) file past. You can easily spot the ones who have never flown before. They look around in awe and amazement as they walk through the business cabin. You can hear them talking to their friends about how beautiful the aircraft is. As they get into the economy section, the squeals of delight are replaced by moans of pain! OK, so I'm exaggerating a little, but the principle is the same! So what's the difference? Well, apart from the free champagne before take-off, the business class seats are wider and there is more leg-room (usually around 40in seat pitch). Normally, in the business cabin of a 747, the seats are seven abreast — two on the fuselage side of the aisles and three in the centre section. In the main cabin, they are normally 10 abreast — three outside the aisles and four in the centre. Most business seats these days incorporate a foot-rest (which always make me feel as if both my legs have been amputated after a couple of hours) and they recline further (around 8°) than those in the main cabin. At an average ratio of 1:15, there are more cabin attendants per seat in business class, the theory being that service is better when, in actual practice, it just means that there are more of them squeezed into the galley having a chat than there are down the back. The food is better in business class too. Instead of getting everything on one tray, it is served like a conventional meal with hors d'oeuvres first, followed by the main course, followed by the dessert and cheese and biscuits, etc. The problem here is that it takes ages to serve a meal and you'll be lucky to finish one in under two

I THINK THEY'RE ON TO ME - SOMEONE'S LOCKED THE DRINKS CABINET AGAIN!

hours. In fact, the marketing people have pulled a real flanker here. The latest trend is to offer, as an option in business class, a so-called 'executive meal' which is aimed at the businessman who needs to spend a relatively short time on his or her meal so that they can get some work done. This 'executive meal' consists of exactly what you would get in the cheaper seats at the back! Everything on one tray. How do they get away with it?

There are also different levels of amenity bag. This is the little thing that you get given to you on almost every flight and contains things like a comb, a flannel, soap, a toothbrush, toothpaste, moisturising cream, aftershave, suicide tablets and the like. In first class they are usually leather and contain Cartier or Chanel perfumes. In business class they are quite nice cloth affairs with Givenchy or Lancome perfumes whilst, in coach, they are plastic with a mineral water splash-on! I've got so many of these darn amenity bags that it's becoming difficult to know where to put them. My wife won't let me throw them away because she's convinced that, one day, she'll find a use for all the rubbish that's in them. I've probably got more in stock right now than British Airways, so if anyone from the world's favourite airline is reading this and would like to make me an offer, then let's do lunch.

So what else can I tell you about business class? Well, you normally get on to, and off the plane before the economy passengers (but after first class passengers of course). In many cases, you can use airline lounges before departure, you get your own check-in desk which is a lot less crowded than the main economy check-in, and you get to look down on the economy passengers in the same way that the first class passengers are looking down on you. That's about it. Oh yes, I nearly forgot. It costs a hell of a lot more and gets you there no quicker. As Greavsie would say — 'Funny old world isn't it?'

Cabin Attendants (see also *Airlines, Business Class, Economy Class, First Class*)

They used to be called air hostesses. I suppose it was something to do with women's lib that forced the change of name to something more asexual. I have no idea what the attendants themselves think of the name, but I hate it. Somehow it just hasn't got the same stature attached to it that 'air hostess' had. The old name sounded glamorous, the new one vaguely vulgar and lavatorial. Anyway, who cares what I think?

Cabin attendants come in two basic types. The ones you see in television commercials and the ones that actually work on aircraft. The two types are completely different and I'm very glad they are. The ones on TV don't look as if they've got the first idea how to look after their own mother, never mind a complete stranger! On the whole, cabin attendants these days are of an extremely high standard. They do, of course, vary from airline to airline, but this is more because of cultural differences between countries than courtesy or efficiency. Expect 'over the top and have a nice day' service with a pearly white-toothed smile from the American airlines, coyness with slavish devotion from the oriental operators and

laid-back good-natured humour from the Aussies. It all depends on your own personal taste.

Frankly, I don't know how they do it. A cabin attendant (whether male or female) has to act as a waiter or waitress, nursemaid, calmer-of-nerves and personal advisor, must have the patience of a saint and acting ability worthy of RADA. All this to be performed in a large aluminium tube! Then there's the antisocial hours that have to be worked, the time-differences to be coped with and constantly living out of suitcases. I know, I know, I sound like the union shop-steward, but I genuinely do admire these people. If it so happens that it gets me better service on my next long-haul, well, that's just the way it is!

Dear Diary. Here is my day. Woke up in the middle of the night and headed for the airport. Got there in plenty of time — the incoming plane was four hours late. Went on board feeling half asleep. Two-thirds of the passengers had got no idea where they were supposed to sit, despite having a boarding card with the seat row and number printed on it. Half the passengers in first class hadn't got enough ice in their drink. The other half had too much. Gave the safety demo for the 4,762nd time. Initial cruising altitude. Time to serve the drinks. Then served more drinks. Then served dinner. Took plenty of verbal abuse from the passengers at the back because everyone at the front wanted chicken and so we had run out. Took the duty-free round. No one had any change and had six arguments about the exchange rate for the rupee. Looked forward to a rest while the film was on, but no such luck. The call button never stopped. Served breakfast. Same hassle again from those at the back. Handed out the landing cards. Most people on the aircraft did not appear to know what nationality they were. Seat belt sign was switched on. Prepared the cabin for landing. Passengers kept getting up. Finally landed. Whilst taxiing, the same people kept getting up. Arrived at the gate. The same people shot out of their seats, formed an instant queue at the door and then moaned when they had to wait for the jetway to be moved into position. Arrived at the hotel for another daylight sleeping session. Looking forward to the same again tomorrow!

Yes, I know they get paid for it and that it was their decision to do the job. I also know that they get to see all sorts of faraway places with strange-sounding names. I still think that they are worth their weight in gold.

Captain (see also *Flightdeck*)

Treat him with respect. Notice I said 'him'. I'm not being sexist, honest. It's just that I can't go all through this section saying 'him or her, he or she' etc. all the time. And although there are thankfully more and more women sitting in the left-hand seat these days, it is still a male-dominated occupation. So when you see a reference to the male gender, please assume that it also applies to the female. Right. That's got that out of the way. The Captain has the power

**The Four Gold Bands
(and lunchbox)
of The Captain**

of life and death over you. You'll recognise him immediately. Apart from looking sickeningly fit, tanned and lean, he will have the standard four gold braids on his sleeve.

By the time you see him striding towards the aircraft, he will already have read the latest notices to airmen, checked the flight plan and learned of the weather conditions *en route*. He may even have eaten a Yorkie bar.

He settles himself into the left-hand seat. No one, incidentally, seems to know for sure why he sits on the left. The usual theory is that, since most of the population is right-handed, it is easier to control the throttle since the levers and most of the buttons, knobs and dials are on his right. Frankly, I don't believe a word of it. My case is built on three facts. Firstly, I'm right-handed, and have no difficulty changing gear in my car. Secondly, the First Officer often does the flying and is usually less-experienced, so why make it more difficult for him by putting him in the right-hand seat? Thirdly, in some of the new fly-by-wire aircraft, the yoke has been reduced to something that looks far more like a computer joystick than something that controls an aircraft, and is placed on the Captain's left! Need I say more? Anyway, I digress. Back to the Captain himself.

He will have started off either flying in the military, or will have obtained a Private Pilot's Licence — around 50hr flying and passing written examinations will get him that far. Then the licence has to be uprated to a Commercial Pilot's Licence. To do that, there are more examinations and around 1,000hr of flying to get in. Then he will need an Instrument Rating. With that lot, if he is lucky, he might be taken on by an airline. Then follows training school, countless hours of simulator training and tutorials, and finally a job in the right-hand seat as First Officer. Eventually he may get command of a smaller aircraft, converting to bigger and better ones in the fullness of time. The end result of all this is the Captain of a Jumbo Jet.

Makes you wonder why they bother, doesn't it? Still, I've heard that the pay's good.

Carousel (see also
Baggage, Lost Property)

Now this device has got to be the invention of the devil! For the uninitiated, a carousel is the official name for the huge cavernous mouth that spews out your precious luggage in the airport at the end of your flight. As the name suggests, they used to be circular. This configuration was, however, soon discarded after it was realised that a circular belt caused hardly any damage to your bags at all. Modern designs are many and varied, but all contain the same basic features such as sharp

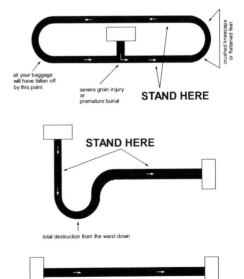

all your baggage will have fallen off by this point

severe groin injury or premature burial

crushed kneecaps or flattened feet

STAND HERE

STAND HERE

total destruction from the waist down

STAND ANYWHERE- BUT BE QUICK!

WAITING AT COMMON TYPES OF CAROUSEL

39

A dreaded baggage carousel at Birmingham Airport. Note the sharp curves designed to amputate at the knee!

bends, which cause your suitcase to teeter precariously before falling off it completely, extremely complicated belt articulating mechanisms, which trap luggage straps before chewing them up, and an ingenious loading method that guarantees your own suitcase always arrives at the bottom of a pile of at least three others!

There is always a great deal of jostling for position at a carousel. Where is pole position? Well, the rules are quite simple. Do not stand too far from the opening of the carousel, or you will be treated to the sight of half of your fellow passengers gleefully mauling your precious case, deciding it is not theirs after all and slinging it back on to the belt. Even worse, one of them might actually walk away with it when you are not looking. It's not their fault really. It's just that either they own a bag that looks just like yours, or they have completely forgotten what their own case looks like! Do not stand near a sharp bend in the belt. This is the place where a large case which has been behaving itself so far, suddenly decides to fight back. You will see it slowly begin to rotate until its sharpest corner is pointing outwards. One of two things will then happen. Either it will suddenly move out when it is directly beside you, hitting a vital part of your anatomy, or it will fall off the belt completely, landing on your foot. Either way, the result as far as you are concerned is the same — immense pain! So wait patiently for your bags on a straight section, somewhere near the feed end. Do not expect to see your cases until at least 400 others have been collected. That way, you will not be disappointed.

Make sure that your luggage has something distinctive about it to aid identification. So many cases are the same these days. Put a multi-coloured belt on it, use a distinctive name tag or paint your name on the bottom. If push comes to shove and you really do not know whether the case in question is yours or not, match up the number of your baggage receipt with the label on the case. Your receipt will be stapled to your ticket. One final thought on the subject — make sure that you do go to the correct carousel. They all display the flight number somewhere near them, so be certain to check that it tallies with the flight that you have just arrived on.

Chartered Aircraft (see also *Airports, Scheduled Flights, Major UK Airports*)

In addition to the scheduled flights, those that operate to a (more or less) fixed timetable, there are numerous chartered aircraft crowding our skies, particularly in summer. The cheap flights that you can book to various holiday destinations are usually on chartered flights. Seats on these aircraft tend to be less expensive for two main reasons. Firstly, the spacing between seats is usually less than on scheduled flights, meaning that more fare-paying passengers can be accommodated. Secondly, these flights only go when there are a sufficient number of passengers booked to ensure that a profit is made. If the airline is committed to the flight, and some seats remain unfilled, they will be sold off cheaply rather than leave them vacant.

It goes without saying that chartered aircraft are subject to exactly the same safety standards as scheduled flights. The service might be more basic, but they will usually get you there just as quickly. If you arrive feeling like you've just been shaken up in a bag full of ferrets — what the hell, you're on holiday!

Check-In (see also *Airports, Baggage Allowance, Dangerous Articles, Hand-Baggage, Latest Check-In Time, Passports, Queues, Seats, Visas*)

This is the first thing that you will want to do when you get to the airport, if only to rid yourself of your increasingly heavy suitcases. Check-in desks for scheduled flights will normally open 2-3hr before departure, but those for charter flights could well be more restricted. Try, if at all possible, to get to the check-in desk reasonably early to be sure of the type of seat that you would like. This is especially important if you have a group of people travelling who would like to be seated together. It is even more important if you would like to sit together in the smoking section, because the number of smoking seats in aircraft has been cut in recent years. The only exception to this general rule is if you hold a confirmed seat assignment. In this case, that seat will be held for you until the latest check-in time printed on your itinerary. After that time, your seat may well be lost and could be offered to a standby passenger.

Make sure that you go to the correct desk. There is nothing more infuriating than queuing for 30 minutes, only to find that you have been standing in the wrong queue! Make sure, therefore, that the sign above the desk is displaying

"WHY CAN'T YOU CARRY A FILOFAX LIKE EVERYONE ELSE ?"

the correct airline, flight number, time of departure and class of travel.

At the desk, you will be asked to produce your ticket. Depending on the type of flight and the airport, you may also be required to show your passport and entrance visa for the country you intend to visit and, in some countries, you will have to pay an airport departure tax, which usually has to be paid in local currency. Make absolutely sure, therefore, that you have enough spending money left over! You will be asked which type of seat you prefer. Smoking (if available on your flight) or non-smoking, aisle, window or centre (if there are centre seats on your aircraft). You can also specify the row number. All this, of course, is subject to availability. So what should you choose? There now follows The Hawkins' Guide To Procuring The Best Seat!

Choose a window seat if you are a sleeper, choose an aisle seat if you have to rush to the loo a lot and choose a centre seat if you have the I.Q. of a boiled mushroom! When choosing a seat, there are, however, other things to be taken into consideration as well. First of all, how tall are you? If you are a six-footer booked into economy class, you are going to be in trouble unless you can get either the front seat in the cabin or one adjacent to an emergency exit. The front seats have a bulkhead in front of them, and always have a little extra leg-room. The emergency exit seats usually have even more leg-room, but it is worthwhile remembering that you will not be able to leave any

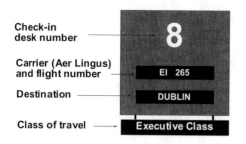

Check-in desk number

Carrier (Aer Lingus) and flight number

Destination

Class of travel

8

EI 265

DUBLIN

Executive Class

INFORMATION ON THE CHECK-IN DESK DISPLAY

hand-luggage on the floor in front of the seat. The route to the exit must, for obvious reasons, remain unobstructed at all times. The same rules apply in business class, although to a lesser extent, since there is more leg-room between seats anyway. If you are travelling first class, you could be wearing stilts and it won't make any difference. There is always one exception, and this has come about only quite recently. On the upper deck of some 747s, there are large box-like containers between the window seats and the fuselage. Apart from being very handy for storing your hand luggage, many people have taken to stretching out their legs on them.

Assuming that you have a free choice of rows, which ones should you go for? Those near the front of the cabin have some advantages. Since the cabin attendants nearly always start serving from the front of each cabin, you will be first in line for the drinks, food and duty-free. You will also be first off the plane and into the immigration queue.

The more safety-conscious amongst you may, on the other hand, choose the rear of the forward cabin or the front of the rear cabin, in order to be as close to the wing-spars as possible. In the event of a crash landing, it is a proven fact that your chances of survival are maximised if you are sitting at the place where the wings join the fuselage. The structure is strongest at this point and more likely, therefore, to remain intact.

Don't pick the rear of the economy cabin if you can avoid it. This area is a long way from the aircraft's centre of gravity and so all movement — up and down (pitching) or side to side (yawing) is magnified. The tail, which is right over your head, tends to act like a giant weathercock in windy conditions and you can find yourself thrown from side to side quite violently on occasion.

Finally, its always a good idea not to sit too close to the

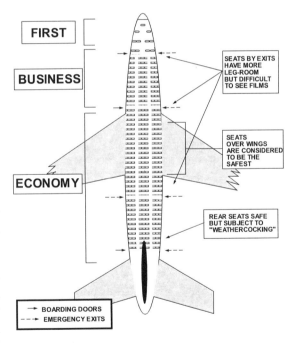

CHOOSING YOUR SEAT ON A WIDE-BODIED JET

(NOT REPRESENTATIVE OF A SEAT PLAN)

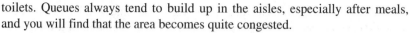

toilets. Queues always tend to build up in the aisles, especially after meals, and you will find that the area becomes quite congested.

So — you have checked in your luggage, chosen your seat and will have been handed your boarding card. Make sure you know which gate your flight is departing from and off you go!

Children

Now don't misunderstand me. I've got two boys of my own who have flown all round the world. I understand the parents' point of view, I really do. That said, I am here to tell you that other people's children on aircraft are a pain in the neck!

There I am, trying to get some sleep, half-drowning in a sea of noise and vomit. Worse yet, someone else's vomit. And why is it that they are always sitting right behind me? Probably because it is the ideal position to kick your backside through the seat, throw up down your neck and scream six inches from your ear!

Airlines try to be very good with children. Most of them have special goodie packs full of crayons and colouring books. If I owned an airline, those bags would include handcuffs, sleeping pills, gags and straitjackets!

The problem is worse on chartered holiday planes, only slightly better in scheduled economy class, much better in business class and unknown in first class. If you can't afford a first class fare, stick a pillow under your backside, drink as much alcohol as you can lay your hands on and pass out. Sweet dreams.

Colds and Flu (see also *Alcohol, Sleeping*)

Flying with a cold can be bloody torture. Here speaks a man of experience. The worst sort by far are head colds, when your nose and ears are completely blocked. All the hassle of flying seems magnified and, by the time you're on board, you're absolutely shattered. But this, dear reader, is but the start of the torture. Take-off. The feeling starts as a dull tingling as the aircraft starts to gain height. The tingling gives way to a pain that starts in the ears and ends in Bangkok! By the time you are a few thousand feet up, you are convinced that your head is going to burst open. You try to swallow to relieve the pressure. It doesn't work. Then your eyes begin to water uncontrollably. A fellow passenger who doesn't fancy the idea of sitting next to a corpse suggests that you try yawning. Normally good advice, but in this case forget it. Finally, you admit defeat and ring the call-button. 'Have you god adythig for a blocked dose ad ears?' you ask in desperation. You may not know it, but you just called the cavalry. A sniff of the evil strong-smelling vapours and you're as good as new. I have no idea what's in the stuff they carry on the aircraft, but

The First Lady takes to the skies.

I'm damn sure that it could wake the dead! The moral of this tale, therefore, is don't suffer in silence if you really have got problems along these lines. Call for a cabin attendant and get sniffing.

It is best, of course, to avoid flying if you have a heavy cold. Everyone knows, however, that this is not always possible. Whether you find yourself having to fly because you have an important business meeting or whether it's because your rented villa in the sun is waiting for you, when you gotta go, you gotta go. Avoid alcohol, take a decongestant before the trip and try to sleep through it if at all possible.

Concorde (see also *Aircraft, Airspeed, First Class, Sound Barrier*)

No A-Z of flying would be complete without a section on 'The First Lady Of The Sky'. Concorde remains, even in the 1990s, the world's only supersonic civil aircraft. That alone makes her something special. But there is something far more exciting about Concorde than mere speed. Although her flight control systems are 'old hat' by today's standards of fly-by-wire and fly-by-light technology, her design is as completely at home in the 1990s as it was in the 1960s. The sleek, slender

Wash the windscreen and fill her up, please Guv!

45

fuselage with its needle nose and delta wings is totally unlike anything else in the sky. In her 'droop snout' configuration for landing, she looks like a vast bird of prey swooping down for a kill. What an aircraft!

Inside Concorde, it is first class all the way. British Airways and Air France consider these wonderful machines to be their flagships and rightly so. Tasteful interiors, wonderful cuisine and celebrity fellow passengers make any scheduled Concorde flight a memorable event. Although anyone used to the spacious interior of a 747 or DC-10 will find Concorde a little cramped inside, this is more than compensated for by the short flight time.

It is unfortunate that Concorde has never lived up to the early expectations of orders from every major world airline, with supersonic routes crossing the world, linking every continent. High operating costs and that tremendous roar from her four Olympus engines have meant that no other airlines have placed orders. Other supersonic airliners under development in the US were scrapped at the drawing board stage, and the Russian 'Concordski' or Tu-144 was withdrawn after a horrific air-display crash. Concorde began to show signs of commercial viability when she was allowed to travel supersonically on the tremendously important transatlantic routes. Today, there is a massive demand for seats on Concorde and, in conjunction with her success as a charter aircraft, she is more popular than ever before.

A scheduled flight on Concorde really is something special. The five-star treatment begins with your arrival at the airport. Check-in is easy and personalised and your baggage is handled for you. Your own departure lounge is right next to the aircraft. The interior of Concorde is first class throughout. You know that you're not in just any old plane the second that Concorde starts take-off roll. A 747 accelerates gently down

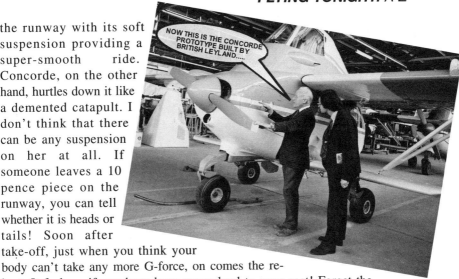

the runway with its soft suspension providing a super-smooth ride. Concorde, on the other hand, hurtles down it like a demented catapult. I don't think that there can be any suspension on her at all. If someone leaves a 10 pence piece on the runway, you can tell whether it is heads or tails! Soon after take-off, just when you think your body can't take any more G-force, on comes the re-heat. It feels as if you have been superglued to your seat! Forget the fairground — this is the place to get your thrills.

Everyone's eyes are on the machmeter at the front of the cabin. Going through the sound barrier is actually something of an anticlimax. You don't feel anything at all. Concorde, unlike other airliners, does not have a fixed cruising altitude. Once she has reached 50,000ft, the throttles are left in a fixed position and she gradually gains height as fuel is burned and she becomes lighter. This is known as the 'cruise-climb' and is the most efficient way to use a jet engine. Normal jetliners cannot take advantage of the cruise-climb efficiency because it would, of course, create mayhem for air traffic controllers. But Concorde, flying at over 50,000ft, happily overtaking high-velocity rifle bullets and the like, has the sky to herself. Apart from some military traffic, which is few and far between, the only thing it has to worry about hitting is another Concorde trundling along in the opposite direction! Because of this, she does not have to be restricted to a fixed flight level in the way that your run-of-the-mill subsonic airliner does. Concorde, therefore, chooses to operate during her cruise in a way that maximises her fuel efficiency. On a normal airliner, the pilot has to compensate for the change in weight as fuel is burned by periodically reducing the throttle settings in order to maintain a constant flight-level for air traffic control purposes.

It is ironic to think that if Concorde had been more successful, and sold to a large number of world airlines, it would have, in turn, been more expensive to run because cruise-climbs would have been banned on safety grounds !

A landing Concorde may look to be in a strange position from the ground, with its nose high and sitting back on its tail, but it feels perfectly normal from inside the cabin. On the ground, the normal formalities are again dealt with quickly and efficiently. A trip across the Atlantic in Concorde simply

The cockpit of Concorde is beginning to show its age. Not a computerised display in sight!

removes all the hassle. You arrive with the feeling that you haven't flown at all. That's what it's all about and why so many prominent businessmen choose to fly Concorde regularly.

The Concorde fleets of Air France and British Airways are getting rather elderly now. Although they are constantly being updated and refitted, they can't go on flying for ever. A lot of people will mourn the passing of this magnificent aircraft.

Contraband (see also *Customs, Duty-Free*)

Ever since I was old enough to remember, I've had a card game called 'Contraband'. The object of the game is to try to keep the money you are given by smuggling the goodies in your hand of cards through customs, rather than declaring them and paying duty. Of course, if you are discovered smuggling, you have to pay a fine to the Customs Officer. There are several items of contraband in the deck. There are bottles of whisky and brandy, cameras, watches, perfume necklaces and - the worst of the lot - The Crown Jewels! Yes, the game is beginning to show its age. No heroin, cocaine, marijuana or opium. No computers or radio cassette recorders. No miniature TVs or

Ork

No Miss - you don't have to declare a tan !

Walkmen. Wasn't life simpler then.

Contraband is, of course, the collective term for any thing brought into the country illegally. This can either be things that are illegal anyway, such as drugs or firearms, or can be legal merchandise that is not declared at customs.

My only advice on carrying contraband is - don't! Customs men seem to have the ability to sniff out suspicious characters as easily as us lesser mortals tell red lights from green. God only knows how they are trained! My advice, incidentally, is further increased in intensity when it comes to smuggling into, or out of, foreign airports. Just think of the film 'Midnight Express'?

Customs (see also *Contraband, Duty-Free Allowances*)

No, not how to hold your fork in polite circles in Afghanistan. It's much more sinister than that. Anything to declare and all that.

I don't know about you but I hate going through the green customs channel when I'm coming back into the UK even when I've only got my regulation cigarettes and bottle. You just immediately feel guilty. How can anyone look casual? There you are, loaded with suitcases, walking past a row of customs officers who are all staring at you. It's hardly a natural situation is it? Do you ignore them and stare straight ahead? Do you start a 'who can stare the longest' contest? Do you look around, not at anyone in particular? I don't know. Since it's such an unnatural situation, I suppose that it's impossible to act naturally in it. The only consolation, of course, is that everybody else is in exactly the same position as yourself and look as guilty as you!

In fact, I hardly ever get stopped and my baggage searched, so I suppose that the customs people must be trained to expect the shifty looks!

It looks innocent enough. They're there somewhere, though, waiting to ambush you!

Dangerous Articles (see also *Bombs, Customs, Hand-Baggage*)

There are many types of dangerous article that are banned from aircraft for obvious safety reasons. If your granny is carrying a flick-knife, or any other form of weapon for that matter, she must declare them at check-in. She can be prosecuted for not doing so.

Needless to say, explosives of any kind are forbidden on aircraft. That includes fireworks, Christmas crackers and even caps for toy guns. Also on the danger list are cylinders of compressed gas, including aqualungs. If you plan to take any aerosols with you, such as hairspray or deodorant, two containers of maximum size 500ml is normally all that you can get away with. They should also be carried in your hand-baggage.

The new generation of butane-powered gas hair curlers are normally OK. Again, pack them in your hand-luggage. Refills, however, are normally banned.

Anything that can easily catch fire or burn is a definite no-no. Lighter fuel, paints and thinners, fire lighters and ordinary matches will not be allowed. Safety matches and cigarette lighters are fine, but objections might be raised if you are carrying more than is necessary for your journey.

Other problem items include bleaches, weed-killer, irritants (although children are allowed), infectious substances, radioactive materials, corrosives such as caustic soda or acid (car type) batteries, magnets or anything containing mercury.

You might be surprised to see magnets on the list. The reason for their appearance is that they can upset the aircraft's navigational systems and send

Never believe the scheduled departure time!

the pilot way off course.

Finally, any electrical items that you are carrying should be declared at check-in. You must also be prepared to switch on any calculator, radio, cassette recorder, computer or whatever, to show that it works as it should.

Delays (see also *Air Traffic Control, Departure Slot, Weather*)

"Mechanics are trained to spot any minor problem, no matter how technical"

Anyone who has flown a few times will almost certainly have been subjected to delays at one stage or another. Both delays in departure and in arrival are quite common these days and seem to be an inevitable result of the greatly increased demand for air travel that the past few years has seen.

Departure and arrival delays are closely linked. The former are often the result of an arrival delay in that the incoming aircraft does not arrive on time and so inevitably it is late in leaving. Even if an aircraft arrives on time for its scheduled departure, there are still many things that can go wrong which can result in a delay. It could be that some passengers who have checked-in for the flight have not made it to

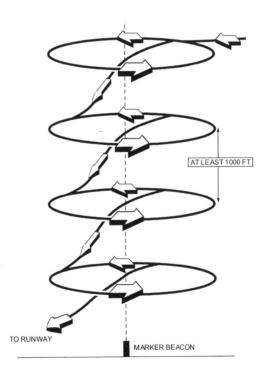

AT LEAST 1000 FT

TO RUNWAY

MARKER BEACON

THE STACKING SYSTEM

51

the departure gate, in which case every attempt will be made to find them and get them on the aircraft before departure. If this is not possible, a further delay will result since the items of baggage that have been checked-in by the non-showing passengers must be located and off-loaded from the aircraft. This is because an airline is not allowed to carry bags without an accompanying passenger for obvious security reasons. Locating the correct items of baggage on a crowded 747 can be a lengthy procedure and it is quite normal for all passengers to disembark and wait in the gate holding area whilst the search is being conducted.

Mechanical problems can also result in lengthy delays. During the pre-flight check of the aircraft, it is more common than most people realise for minor faults to show up, which have to be corrected before take-off. Small delays can often become much longer ones in these days of very crowded skies. If a pilot misses his take-off slot for whatever reason, even though he may only be two or three minutes late, that slot will have been taken by someone else and he may well find himself having to wait for an hour or more for a new one. This is a result of air traffic control restrictions being applied to ensure safety of travel.

Delays can also come about as a result of poor weather conditions, either at the departure airport or along the scheduled flight path, when new flight plans will have to be filed to avoid large storms, strong winds or the like.

On the whole, when you consider the number of things that can go wrong, I think that it is quite remarkable that so many aircraft depart at, or very close to, their scheduled time.

Arrival delays can, in turn, be a direct result of departure delays. Additionally, they may be caused by a longer than usual flying time, resulting from storm-avoiding routes or severe head winds. Occasionally, if a route is lengthened considerably, it will be necessary to make an unscheduled refuelling stop *en route*, which will always put back an arrival time by at least one to one and a half hours. Perhaps the most infuriating arrival delay is when the aircraft arrives in the vicinity of the airport on time, but is then made to fly around in circles in a stack for what seems like eternity, before being given a landing slot. Again, I'm afraid that this is a result of the large number of aircraft now in our skies and the rate at which aircraft can land on a runway and still leave a good safety margin. The frustration here is compounded if you are hoping to catch a connecting flight. On many occasions, I have spent 30 minutes to an hour flying in circles, only to see my connecting flight take off from an adjacent runway as I am landing.

Delays tend to be worst in summer, when large numbers of holidaymakers and charter aircraft increase airport congestion to often ridiculous levels.

Even if you know that your flight is going to be delayed, you must still report to the check-in desk at the airport by the latest time printed on your itinerary or ticket. If you do not, your seat may well be assigned to someone else.

This is as far as you'll get if you forget your passport.

Departure Lounge (see also *Airports*)

This animal varies greatly from airport to airport around the world. It can be anything from a spacious and comfortable area, well endowed with seats and refreshment amenities to a glorified cattle-pen; a holding area for bemused passengers desperately waiting for their flights to depart.

No matter how well appointed, the departure lounge may be quite a shock to the system. It is normally teeming with people, no seats are available and hordes of little children are roaming around looking for some poor sod who deserves ice-cream down the front of his shirt!

Your first sight of the departure lounge will be when you have just cleared passport control, after which there is no going back. The first thing you should consider, therefore, is when to go through. Ask what amenities are available on 'the other side' when you are checking-in. If the departure lounge sounds absolutely dreadful, simply wait on the check-in side of the airport until you really have to go through. Do not, however, leave it until the last minute. Always be prepared for queues when you least expect them.

As a general rule, unless you are leaving a Third World country, or an airport that has simply not been able to keep up with increased demand, the departure lounge will be perfectly acceptable. Bear in mind, of course, that all lounges will be far busier in the middle of the holiday season. The exception seems to be Gatwick, where the 'silly season' never stops. No sooner have the St Moritz brigade hung up their skis for another year when the Benidorm bunch are out in force, getting nicely lubricated and falling over the little kids with the ice-creams. It's just the same at three o'clock in the morning!

In addition to all this mayhem, the departure lounge usually contains duty-free shops, newsagents, snack-bars and the all-important departure indicator

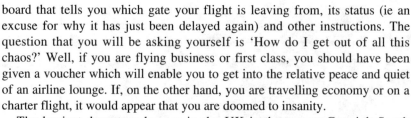

board that tells you which gate your flight is leaving from, its status (ie an excuse for why it has just been delayed again) and other instructions. The question that you will be asking yourself is 'How do I get out of all this chaos?' Well, if you are flying business or first class, you should have been given a voucher which will enable you to get into the relative peace and quiet of an airline lounge. If, on the other hand, you are travelling economy or on a charter flight, it would appear that you are doomed to insanity.

The busiest departure lounge in the UK is the one at Gatwick South Terminal. It is not really a lounge at all, just an area with a few seats in the middle of the shops. It is always absolutely packed, usually with standing room only. If you find yourself departing from the South Terminal, my advice is to wait in the 'Satellite', regardless of whether your flight is leaving from it or not. You will see direction signs for the Satellite in the lounge. It is a small circular mini-terminal, linked to the main terminal by an automatic monorail train which leaves every two minutes and takes only a minute or so to get there. You will find that the Satellite will be a lot less crowded than the main terminal and it is fully equipped with its own duty-free shop and snack-bars. It is certainly a far more pleasant place to be in than the main departure lounge. The only problems with waiting in the Satellite are firstly that your flight departure will not be announced from there if is not leaving from the Satellite, and secondly, you will have to go through a security check when returning to the main departure lounge. This is, however, a little price to pay for the peace of the Satellite.

If you are unlucky enough to find yourself having to spend several hours in a departure lounge because your flight is inordinately delayed, buy a thick paperback and get engrossed in it. Every hour or so, for a break, go and have a cup of coffee or just put your book down and watch the world go by. That in itself can be very entertaining — you see some strange characters wandering about in airport departure lounges!

Departure Slot (see also *Air Traffic Control, Delays*)

You will quite often find yourself sitting in an aircraft at the departure gate, doors having been closed, the jetway removed and nothing else happening. This is usually because the pilot is waiting for his departure slot, the time at which he has been told by air traffic control that he can take off. For reasons of economy, the captain will not normally start his engines until shortly before his allotted take-off time.

Departure slots have to be booked some time in advance and the problem is that if, for some reason, your aircraft misses its allocated slot, it may well have to wait for a relatively long time before being given another one. This problem is more severe during the height of the summer, when airports are much busier with holiday traffic. It would seem that very little can be done about this problem. Building more airports is not the answer, as the problem of over-crowded flight lanes would not be resolved. The complexities involved in keeping hundreds of aircraft, flying dozens of different routes, at a safe distance from each other in the skies are such that it is difficult to see how the problem will ever be overcome.

Departure Tax

At some airports around the world a charge is made by the airport authority for using it on departure. This charge is referred to as the departure tax and is collected, as a rule, at the time of check-in. You will not be able to leave the airport without paying the tax and obtaining the official receipt. It is often the case that payment of this tax must be made in cash and in local currency. Always ensure, therefore, that you have sufficient cash left over from your trip to avoid what could well be very lengthy delays at the bureau de change. It is always a good idea to check well beforehand whether or not the airport you intend to use levies a departure tax.

Departure Time (see also *Delays, Estimated Time of Arrival, Latest Check-In Time*)

Not to be confused with the time the aircraft actually takes off, this is a myth-ical time invented by the airlines to get you to the airport when they want you to be there. Even if everything goes completely according to plan, you will be lucky if the crew are closing the aircraft doors at 'departure time'. After that, assuming that the captain still has a departure slot, you will have to leave the ramp, taxi to the end of the runway and take your place in the queue for take-off. It will be a miracle if your wheels leave the tarmac earlier than 30min after 'departure time'. The only exception to this general rule is if you are flying from a very small airport which is little used by other traffic.

Don't worry too much about it, though. Pilots are extremely good at making up time *en route*, so just because you are late taking off it does not mean that you will be late in arriving.

Disasters (see also *Bombs*)

Thankfully, they don't happen often, but when they do, they are big news. Because of the attention the media gives to even the slightest aircraft incident, it is all too easy to blow out of all proportion the risk of encountering a disaster whilst flying. No one is going to tell you about the thousands and thousands of flights that take place every day without incident!

Disasters tend to fall into five basic categories. These are: 1) Mechanical Faults, 2) Pilot Error, 3) Bad Weather, 4) Traffic Control Errors, 5) Terrorist Activity.

D

We'll have a look at each of these types separately. Some, of course, have been caused by a combination of problems, so it is impossible to fit them entirely in one category. The aim is not to scare the would-be passenger half to death, but rather to show how knowledge of each type of problem is now so good that preventive measures taken these days keep the risks down to an absolute minimum.

1) Mechanical Faults

This group can be further sub-divided into faults resulting from bad aircraft design and those that stem from poor maintenance. The series of Comet crashes in the 1950s led to a much greater understanding of metal fatigue and fuselage strength. The project was a bold one — to develop an aircraft that would fly twice as fast at twice the height of conventional aircraft. To do this, new aerodynamics and flying control systems were required. Completely new metal bonding techniques were needed to produce a strong yet lightweight construction, whilst the fuselage would be subjected to higher stress levels than had been previously encountered. The first production Comet flew in 1951 and carried 36-44 passengers at Mach 0.74. The first variant, the Comet 2, had an extended fuselage for greater payload and range. In 1952, the Comet 3 with even greater range was announced. Less than six months after the inaugural flight, a Comet was lost on take-off at Rome. The accident was attributed to pilot error. In the same year, another Comet crashed on take-off, this time at Karachi. The cause was again determined as pilot error. In 1953, a Comet disintegrated in flight at 10,000ft in a tropical storm *en route* to Delhi. Failure of the port elevator spar was said to have caused the loss of this aircraft. In 1954, a French Comet overshot the runway at Dakar and, in the same year, a Comet departing Rome broke up at 27,000ft. The cause was never established. Two weeks later another Comet *en route* to Cairo disintegrated at 30,000ft. Not until after this latter disaster were Comets grounded. A lengthy investigation proved that the cabins of these aircraft were prone to metal fatigue, especially at the

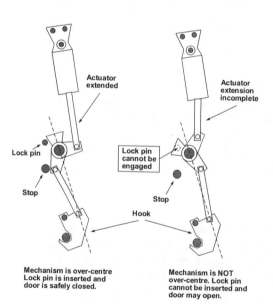

Actuator extended

Actuator extension incomplete

Lock pin

Lock pin cannot be engaged

Stop

Stop

Hook

Mechanism is over-centre Lock pin is inserted and door is safely closed.

Mechanism is NOT over-centre. Lock pin cannot be inserted and door may open.

THE DC-10 REAR CARGO DOOR LOCK

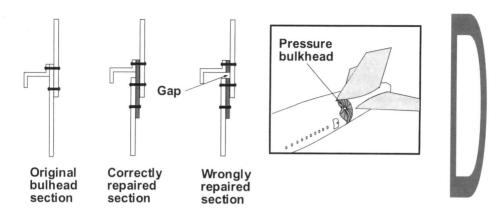

Original
bulhead
section

Correctly
repaired
section

Wrongly
repaired
section

Gap

Pressure
bulkhead

THE REAR PRESSURE BULKHEAD REPAIR PROBLEM ON THE 747

corners of cabin windows and the ADF aerial window. After modification, Comets 4, 4B and 4C provided excellent service around the world for 25 years.

The problem that emerged with the rear cargo door of the DC-10 in the mid-1970s proved that what was thought to be a failsafe mechanical lock and indicator simply wasn't foolproof. American Airlines' flight 96 departed Detroit in June that year for Buffalo. The groundcrew had reported trouble closing the rear cargo door, which blew out at 12,000ft. Thankfully, the pilot managed an emergency landing at Detroit, using only the throttle controls of numbers one and three engines for control of the aircraft. The control cables and the throttle linkage to the number two tail engine had been destroyed by the floor collapsing when decompression occurred. Modifications were made to the actuators which closed the door electrically to ensure the latch was safely driven over-centre. In this position, lock-pins could be engaged and the door was safe. In the case of flight 96, the latch was not over-centre and the lock-pins had been bent against a securing flange. A peephole was incorporated so that a visual check of the correct pin positioning could be made. In March 1974, however, Turkish Airlines' flight 981 was on the ground at Paris. The cargo door latch was not locked over-centre and the peephole was not checked. Shortly after take-off, at 11,500ft, the door blew out. The rear cabin floor collapsed into the cargo section, two rows of seats were ejected and the elevators and rudder jammed. Just over a minute later, the aircraft hit the ground, disintegrated and killed all 346 on board. Shortly afterwards, the rear floor on the DC-10 was strengthened so that it could withstand the pressure of a cargo door blow-out.

The failure of an engine/pylon structure on an American Airlines DC-10 caused a disaster at Chicago in 1979. Two seconds before becoming airborne, after the speed at which the aicraft is committed to take off, the left wing engine and pylon detached completely and hurtled into the runway. Flight controls were jammed and a slat retracted, causing the port wing to stall. After half a minute of flight, the aircraft came down, killing everyone aboard. Later inspections revealed that damage had been caused to the pylons of other DC-10s whose engines had been removed for maintenance. All DC-10s worldwide were grounded until the matter was resolved.

All of these can be attributed, in part at least, to flaws in design, although it must also be said that incorrect maintenance or operating procedures certainly contributed. The loss of a 747, Japan Airlines' flight 123, in 1985 between Tokyo and Osaka is now known to be a result of improper maintenance procedures, when a repair to the rear pressure bulkhead was not carried out in accordance with the manufacturer's instructions and blew out in mid-flight. The resulting blast of air pressurised the tailfin, destroying half of it, and damaged control cables to the elevator and rudder. The aircraft went into an uncontrollable Dutch Roll and eventually hit a mountain and broke up. Only four survived.

2) Pilot Error

Perhaps the most emotive of all categories, because it involves human competence, is that of pilot error. Disasters happen for this reason simply because anyone, including a pilot, can make a mistake, particularly in times of heightened activity or stress. The Trident crash near Heathrow in 1972, the Air New Zealand crash at Mount Erebus near the South Pole in 1979 and the British Midland Airways crash on the M1 near East Midlands Airport were all attributable, to one degree or another, to pilot error. The BEA Trident departed Heathrow's Runway 28R for Brussels whilst over the payload limit, but below the maximum take-off weight because of the low amount of fuel being carried.

STALLING IN A HIGH-TAILED AIRCRAFT:
1. The engine intakes are in the area of turbulent flow from the stalled wings.

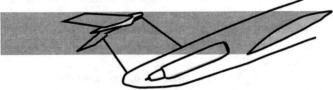

2. The Deep stall. The Elevators are in the area of turbulent flow and are therefore inoperative.

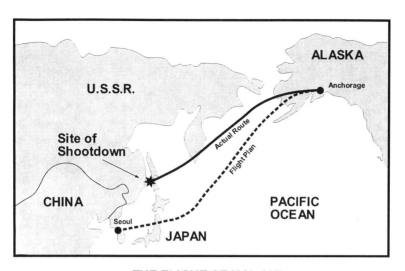

THE FLIGHT OF KAL 007

The droops, a wing feature peculiar to the Trident, were set in during the initial climb, but the tailplane was set for the droops being out. The aircraft was, therefore, trimmed for a stall. The stall caused the plane to lose height and, passing down through 1,200ft, the aircraft entered a deep stall, where the elevators fall into the area of turbulent airflow and recovery is impossible. The aircraft fell with its nose 31° up and its airspeed only 54kts. The situation became even worse as the plane broke through the cloud at 1,000ft with its nose 60° up and it disintegrated on impact with the ground.

In the case of the Mount Erebus collision near the South Pole, a series of ground errors caused the Inertial Navigation System to be in error and direct the aircraft towards the mountain. Despite poor visibility, the Captain elected to continue with this sightseeing tour from Auckland and hit the lower slopes of the mountain. All aboard were killed. The sightseeing trips were discontinued after the crash.

Incorrect readings from the Inertial Navigation System due to pilot error are also thought to be the reason for the accidental shooting down of Korean Airlines' flight 007 by the Soviets in 1983. The flight was on the ground at Anchorage, Alaska, during a scheduled stop between New York and Seoul. At Anchorage, the INS was set to the alignment mode, when the co-ordinates of the aircraft's present position, together with those of the way-points and destination, must be keyed in. This has to be performed three times, since there are three separate INS computers. After the data has been inserted, the aircraft must remain perfectly still for around 13 minutes, as the INS platforms stabilise. The flight began to deviate from its correct course almost immediately, and passed 12 miles north of the first way-point. This was, apparently, unnoticed by the crew, who continued to report good progress. By the way-point known as Nippi, the aircraft was 185 miles off course. This took flight 007 over Sakhalin Island, a site of Soviet secret military installations. A Sukhoi Su-15 fighter was sent to intercept the plane, which was probably wrongly identified as an American KC-135 spy plane which had recently been flying in the area to test Soviet defences. The fighter fired two rockets, destroying the Korean Airliner, which hit the sea west of Sakhalin Island, killing all 269 aboard. At the time of interception, the 747 was 365 miles from its correct position. It is thought that either the aircraft was moved from the ramp in Anchorage before the gyros had stabilised, or the wrong co-ordinates for the ramp were fed in. Interestingly, it has been shown that an error in just one digit leads to the shootdown point, although it must be remembered that this wrong data would have to be fed in on three separate occasions.

Collisions with high ground continue to be a major cause of crashes. Over or under-shooting the runway still happens, and instruments continue to be incorrectly set or misread. Modern avionics systems, however, have greatly reduced the chances of this sort of thing taking place. Ground warning proximity systems, with their speech synthesisers, tell the crew if the aircraft is flying too low. Computers cross-checking each other for discrepancies and the new type of electronic instrumentation and head-up displays have led to fewer perception errors. Still, though, pilot error continues. Some consider that it is simply because too much is being asked of the flight crew. In addition to the problems of jet-lag causing disorientation, during a typical flight the cockpit will be a scene of high activity during take-off and landing, with very little happening in between. The automated nature of the flight at cruising altitude can lead to boredom. If an emergency develops, and manual action is necessary, the crew will have to react very quickly. Rapid problem diagnosis and remedial action demands an alert mind. It is difficult to stay alert when 90% of the flight requires no action from the crew apart from regular reporting to the ground and routine adjustments. Perhaps we will never be able to completely eliminate pilot error as long as we have human pilots. And I, for one, do not fancy the idea of flying around the world with only a machine on the flight-deck. I don't care how clever it is!

3) Bad Weather

In the early days of flying, bad weather was always one of the main causes of aircraft loss. Aircraft before the advent of the jet engine lacked both the ability to detect storms ahead and to fly above them in clear non-turbulent air. The modern jet airliner has a variety of techniques to help avoid virtually all unpleasant weather systems. In addition to satellite maps being available before the flight, and regular updates being provided by air traffic control, the pilot also has sophisticated on-board weather radar. This will show him turbulent weather systems further along his route, in plenty of time for him to be able to take evasive action.

Again, in the early days of civil flight, low cloud levels, leading to poor visibility on the landing approach, were a major cause of disasters. Modern airliners are equipped with computerised instrument landing systems (ILS) which can do the pilot's job for him in zero visibility.

The main weather-related threat to safety in modern aircraft is probably ice. When ice forms on the wings, the ability of that wing to produce lift is seriously reduced. This led to the crash in the Potomac River of an Air Florida aircraft outbound from the National Airport in Washington DC. Although de-icing had been carried out on the aircraft prior to departure, it was forced to wait for so long in the take-off queue that ice reformed both on the wings and in the airspeed detector tube. The resulting false airspeed readings and poor wing performance led to an attempted take-off before enough lift had been generated for flight.

Ice is rarely a problem in flight in modern aircraft, because the leading edge of the wing, which is electrically heated in any case, is warmed by friction as it forces its way through the air. The height at which a jet flies also reduces the risk of icing, since the relative humidity is low.

Ice on runways is now dealt with by modern de-icing technology which keeps airports open for business in all but the most appalling weather conditions. The safety margins for ice, snow and slush on a runway were modified after the Munich disaster of 1958, involving the Manchester United football team. Runway 25 was covered with 20mm of slush. After two aborted take-offs due to engine problems, the aircraft actually decelerated after achieving V1 due to the braking effect of the slush. The plane ran out of runway and hit a house, killing 23.

There is no doubt that an airliner's ability to fly safely in bad weather has increased remarkably in the last 20 years or so. Thunderstorms, low-level cloud, rain and ice, once considered to be killers in the air, are now regarded as mere inconveniences.

4) Traffic Control Errors

Air traffic control is a complicated business, and getting more complicated every day. Although it is superbly efficient when one considers the number of aircraft that are handled around the world every day, mistakes can, and do, happen. The mid-air collision is now part of our vocabulary. Although this can also be a result of pilot error, several collisions have been attributed directly to errors on the part of an overworked and inattentive controller. The 1976 mid-air collision over Yugoslavia is an example. A BEA Trident, *en route* to Istanbul from Heathrow and a Yugoslavian charter plane from Split, heading for Cologne, converged over Zagreb. The Trident was in the upper flight sector whilst the Yugoslavian aircraft was flying through the mid sector. Air traffic control erroneously gave the latter permission to climb to Flight Level 350 (35,000ft) in the upper layer. The mistake was recognised shortly afterwards and the Yugoslavian plane was told by the controller to hold at

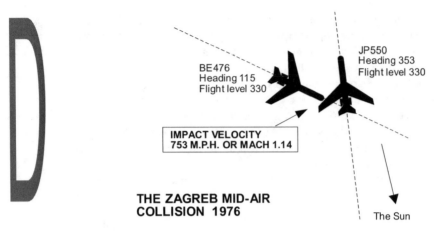

BE476
Heading 115
Flight level 330

JP550
Heading 353
Flight level 330

**IMPACT VELOCITY
753 M.P.H. OR MACH 1.14**

**THE ZAGREB MID-AIR
COLLISION 1976**

The Sun

Level 330, believing the Trident to be at Level 335. It was, in fact, also at Level 330 and the two aircraft collided, the Yugoslavian DC-9 port wing slicing through the flightdeck of the Trident. The flight crew aboard the Trident were killed instantly. The wing of the DC-9 broke off and the debris was sucked into the port engine which disintegrated. There were no survivors.

Unfortunately, aircraft collisions on the ground are becoming more common, although many airports have now installed ground radar to help them handle large volumes of traffic on runways, taxiways and aprons. The worst aviation disaster ever is an example of what can happen when there is no ground radar and visibility is poor, although there was an element of pilot error in what transpired on Sunday, 27 March 1977 at Los Rodeos Airport, Tenerife. Two 747s, Pan American flight PA 1736 and KLM's KL 4805, were diverted there from Las Palmas because of a bomb which had exploded earlier. Fog was beginning to engulf the airport and the runway centre-lights

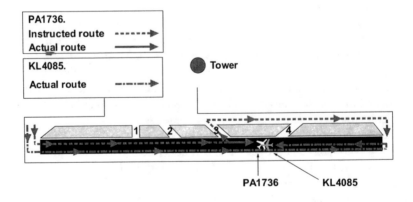

PA1736.
Instructed route - - - - - ➤
Actual route ———➤

KL4085.
Actual route - - · - · - ➤

Tower

1 2 3 4

PA1736   KL4085

THE TENERIFE DISASTER 1977

were out of service. KL 4805 was told by the ground controller to taxi along the single runway and backtrack for take-off. Meanwhile, PA 1736 was instructed to taxi along the runway and exit at taxiway Number 3. The 747 missed the exit as KL 4805 began its take-off roll before receiving final permission. The KLM aircraft had reached V1 when the pilot of the Pan American aircraft saw him. The latter tried to turn left off the runway and the KLM pilot tried to take off over him. There was, however, not enough time for PA 1736 to clear the runway and KL 4805 had insufficient airspeed for flight. The latter landed on top of the former and both aircraft broke up and caught fire. Of the 396 passengers on PA 1736, 335 died. All 248 aboard KL 4805 were killed.

5) Terrorist Activity

This is a category that belongs very much to the modern age. Terrorists can, and do, strike in airports and aircraft themselves. It began with hijacking, which seemed to reach a peak in the 1970s, when 'Fly me to Cuba' became part of our everyday language. Stricter controls on the smuggling of firearms and grenades, coupled with the relatively low success rate for terrorists operating in this way, has since led to a reduction in the number of hijackings that take place. The hijacking threat has, however, been replaced by a much more sinister one. The bomb. Everyone remembers the Lockerbie disaster, in which a 747, PanAm flight 103, was brought down over the Scottish town by an altitude-triggered explosive: the bomb, which contained the terrorists' favourite weapon — Semtex — was hidden in a portable radiocassette and was not detected either when loaded on to its original plane or when transferred to the 747. It is not known how many more disasters have been caused by bombs because the attack is normally planned to take place whilst the aircraft is over deep water to hide any evidence. This appears to be what happened in the case of the Air India 747 loss of 1985 off the Irish coast.

New explosive detectors are now in use and even more sophisticated ones are under development. It is now much more difficult to smuggle bombs on to aircraft. New regulations now mean that no items of personal baggage can be carried aboard a passenger aircraft without the owner of the bags travelling with them. Hopefully, bombs on aircraft will soon be a thing of the past.

Each of the disasters described has, in some way, led to modifications to aircraft or operating procedures. Although it is a terrible thing that lessons have to be learned in this way, the skies are now much safer and flying continues to be the safest way to travel.

Drinking (see also *Alcohol*)

The golden rule is — water, good — alcohol, bad!

Don't take it too literally. A well-diluted spirit, a glass of wine or a beer isn't going to kill you and will make you feel relaxed if you are a nervous sort or ease the monotony if you get bored quickly. But don't be silly about it. Don't drink yourself into a stupor just because it's free. And remember, if you are drunk on board and causing a problem, the Captain has every right to divert his aircraft and put you off at the first available airport. That is going to cost the airline a lot of money. Guess who they'll be looking to for compensation. Full marks!

Dutch Roll (see also *Pitch, Roll, Yaw*)

No — not something that you get for breakfast on KLM. Being in an aircraft which is in a Dutch Roll is not, thankfully, something that you are likely to experience. An aircraft is said to be performing a Dutch Roll when it is rolling

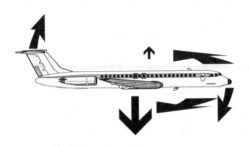

THE DUTCH ROLL

(wings moving up and down), pitching (nose tipping up and down) and yawing (nose moving from side to side) all at the same time. As I am sure you can imagine, this is a very uncomfortable motion and one very likely to make you feel sick in a very short time!

An aircraft would normally only go into a Dutch Roll when the flight controls are not working, such as happened in the Japan Airlines' 747 crash of 1985. In this case, the hydraulic lines that operate the ailerons, elevators and rudder were destroyed.

A total mystery to me is exactly why it is called a 'Dutch Roll'. I sincerely hope that it is not a comment on the ability of pilots from The Netherlands to make clean turns!

Duty-Free (see also *Duty-Free Allowances, Customs, Hand-Baggage*)

When travelling between two separate countries, you are usually allowed to go through the age-old ritual known as 'the purchase of duty-free'. This involves buying, either in the airport you are leaving, or on board the aircraft, your allocation of duty-free booze, cigarettes or gifts. These can then, provided you have not exceeded your quota, be imported into the country of arrival without having to pay duty on them. Most people tend to make their selection from the duty-free stores at the airports, which are located inside the departure area. In most airports, the duty-free shops operate as normal supermarkets and you make your purchases there and then. You will need to show your boarding card to the cashier, as proof that you are intending to leave the country. Do make sure that you have a close look at the prices of duty-free items — they are not always the bargains that they appear to be. Also make sure that you are not buying more than your duty-free allowance of the country that you are visiting. The allowances vary from country to country and you will need to check your entitlement beforehand. Please remember that you are not allowed to open your duty-free goods or consume them before you are out of the country in which they were purchased.

The site of the ancient ceremony known as 'The purchase of the duty-free'.

Duty free-goods can also be bought in-flight and are often cheaper on aircraft than in the airports. There is, however, a much narrower selection of items available and it is quite common not to be able to get hold of your favourite brand of cigarette or whisky.

Whichever way you look at it, it seems to be absolutely ridiculous that aircraft fly all over the world, loaded with bottles of alcohol, cigarettes and other goods for duty-free purchase. In addition to this increasing the all-up weight of the aircraft and therefore its operating economy, there has to be a real risk that, in the event of an accident, flying bottles of alcohol could cause serious damage. It has always seemed to me to be far more sensible that duty-free items be purchased on arrival in the country, rather than having to trans-port them from the country of departure by air. I understand that this idea has, in fact, been adopted as a trial scheme in a couple of places around the world and, as far as I am aware, seems to be working satisfactorily.

When going through customs on arrival, provided that you have no more than your duty-free allowance, you will not need to declare your goods.

Duty-Free Allowances (see also *Customs*)

When coming into the UK, there are two allowance bands for goods. Provided that the allowances in a band are not exceeded, no tax will be charged. The first band is for goods obtained anywhere outside the EU, or for goods obtained duty-free within the EU from a duty-free shop. The second band is for goods obtained duty and tax paid within the EU, provided that they are for your own personal use.

It is always wise to check with HM Customs and Excise if you are in any

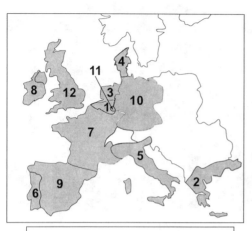

1. BELGIUM	7. FRANCE
2. GREECE	8. IRISH REPUBLIC
3. THE NETHERLANDS	9. SPAIN
4. DENMARK	10.GERMANY
5. ITALY	11.LUXEMBOURG
6. PORTUGAL	12.U.K.

THE COUNTRIES OF THE E.C.

doubt about your entitlement. However, at the time of writing, the allowances are:

Duty-Free

Tobacco — 200 cigarettes or 100 cigarillos or 50 cigars or 250g of tobacco

Wine — 2 litres of still table wine

Alcohol — 1 litre of spirits or strong liqueurs (over 22% volume) or 2 litres of fortified or sparkling wine or other liqueurs or 2 additional litres of still table wine.

Perfume — 60ml

Toilet water/Aftershave — 250ml

Gifts etc — £36 worth, but no more than 50 litres of beer.

Duty and Tax Paid

EU Law has set out guide levels. If you exceed these levels, then you must be prepared to prove that all goods are for your own personal use and not for re-selling. The guide levels are:

Cigarettes — 800, Cigarillos — 400, Cigars — 200, Tobacco — 1kg.

Spirits — 10 litres, Fortified Wines — 20 litres, Wine — 90 litres, but not more than 60 litres sparkling, Beer — 110 litres.

Remember that no one under 17 is allowed a tobacco or drinks allowance, so don't bring in a load for the kids as well as yourself!

Duty free allowances for travel within the EU can now be bought on both the outward and return journey, effectively doubling your entitlement.

Just so that you're absolutely certain, although I'm sure you know it already, the countries of the EU are Belgium, Denmark, France, Germany, Greece, Italy, Irish Republic, Luxembourg, The Netherlands, Portugal, Spain (except for The Canaries) and the UK (except for The Channel Isles).

Economy Class (see also *Business Class, First Class, Seats*)

Unless you are Corporate Executive, filthy rich or just plain careless with your money, this is the only part of the aircraft you'll ever sit in. But don't despair, dear reader. It's really rather nice.

The seats are a bit closer together than in business or first class, a wee bit narrower and they don't recline as far (only about 6°). The average seat pitch is about 32in. The food isn't quite as good, and the headphones may sound a little on the tinny side. Service will be a bit slower in the cheap seats, because there are fewer attendants per passenger (average ratio 1:35). It won't be that bad, though. Certainly better than in a good restaurant. The main thing is that you are getting to the same place just as quickly as the others up front but at a much lower cost. Not a bad deal. And if you have something nice to look forward to at the end of the flight, so much the better.

The only snag with economy class is the appearance, in wide-bodied aircraft, of the dreaded centre seat. You'll find this monstrosity insulted in a separate section.

Emergency Evacuations (see also *Emergency Exits, Smoke Hoods*)

The official version of the emergency evacuation sounds like fun. We all stand in a neat queue — no pushing or shoving — and individually slide down the giant inflatable slides at the exits to safety. They charge a fortune for that sort of thing at Alton Towers!

The reality of the situation, however, is a little different. The main danger, it would appear, is fire and smoke. Smoke can be so dense and acrid that visibility is reduced to zero. Panic follows. The floor of a modern jet is equipped with a row of lights which lead the way to an exit, but I have heard of instances when even those have been invisible. Although I am not one of life's pessimists, I always take the advice given to me several years ago by an experienced Captain of a 747.

He told me that the most effective safety measure is, when first occupying your seat, to count the number of seat-backs between you and the nearest exit. That way, even if you can't see anything, you are going to be able to find your way out of a smoke-filled fuselage. The other bit of wisdom is to get as close to the floor as possible. This is where any clear and breathable air is going to be. I'm sure that there would be a lot less panic if smoke hoods were freely available, but that isn't going to happen for some time yet, the way things are going.

So there it is. Try not to panic. Know how to find your exit (and how to open the door) in the dark. Get your face as close to the floor as possible. And enjoy your trip down that slide!

Emergency Exits

As part of the safety briefing before take-off, the position of the emergency exits will be demonstrated. Their

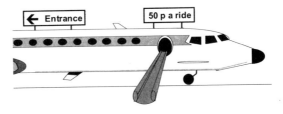

Emergency evacuations sound like fun!

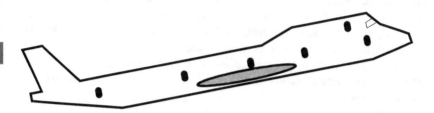

The Emergency exits on a Boeing 747
Some airlines have removed the over-wing exits.

number and position varies from plane to plane, as does their method of operation. Make sure that you know where the nearest exit to your seat is located and look on the safety card in your seat pocket for the operating instructions.

It is usual to have two emergency exits at the front of the aircraft; one on either side, and either one or two at the rear. In addition, most aircraft have extra exits over the wings on either side of the fuselage. A Boeing 747 is manufactured with 10 exits on the main deck and an additional one on the upper deck. Some airlines have, however, elected to remove the two over-wing exits to allow the fitting of more seats. This move was, and still is, opposed by pilots.

During the flight, the doors are put on automatic operation, when they can

It's a good idea to count and remember the number of seat-backs between your seat and the emergency exit.

all be operated from the flightdeck in the event of an emergency. After the aircraft has arrived at its destination and is ready to disembark passengers, the doors are switched to manual.

Some passengers prefer to sit in a seat adjacent to an exit because leg-room is greater, but it is vitally important that no items are placed on the floor in front of these seats. Clearly, they would obstruct the exit in the event of an emergency.

Emergency Landings (see also *Emergency Evacuations*)

Emergency landings are extremely rare, thank heavens. Even so, it is wise to spend a little time before take-off familiarising yourself with the aircraft's interior — just in case. Listen to the safety briefing given by the cabin attendants. Yes, I know that they are as boring as hell and the demonstrators are even more bored than you. But do it just the same. For me. In addition, there are other things that you can do to increase your chances of survival in an emergency. Remember that most emergency evacuations take place in less-than-ideal visibility conditions. Sometimes in the dark and sometimes in smoke-filled cabins. So make sure that you can find your way out in the dark. Practise it mentally. It's a simple technique but it could save your life.

When an emergency landing is expected, you will be told to adopt the brace position. Unfortunately, the brace position demonstrated on the safety cards varies from airline to airline. New research since the Kegworth crash in January 1989 has, however, recently shown that a new brace position could greatly reduce the seriousness and number of injuries resulting from most crash landings. The positions shown on virtually all safety cards call for the legs to lean forwards. Hands are shown either on the back of the seat in front, under the knees or around the head. Particularly dangerous are the ones that ask you to place your hands, with or without your arms crossed, on the top of the seat-back in front of you. During sudden impact, these positions cause the legs to flail forwards under the bottom of the seat in front, often resulting in broken bones. Arms also flail and can be fractured. The head tends to power into the tray mounted in the seat-back, which is obviously quite hard. Spinal injuries can also result. The new position consists of tucking the lower legs back slightly behind the knees, so that there is less tendency for the

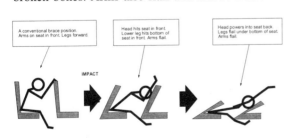

A Conventional brace position, now known to cause damage to head, arms, legs and spine.

legs to shoot forward under the bottom of the seat in front during impact. When this happens, the whole body tends to react violently back and forth, causing damage to the arms, head and torso in addition to the legs and feet. In the

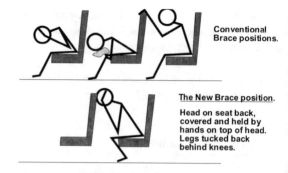

Conventional Brace positions.

The New Brace position.
Head on seat back, covered and held by hands on top of head. Legs tucked back behind knees.

new position, the hands should be placed on top of the head, with the elbows tucked in. The head should be resting on the back of the seat in front. It has been shown that the adoption of this position minimises dangerous flailing of the limbs.

Practise the new position at home. Do it until it is almost instinctive. In a real-life emergency, you may only have a few seconds to get into the brace position.

When the aircraft has come to a halt, it is vital that the cabin is evacuated in the shortest time possible. This does not mean that everyone should rush immediately for the exits. Quite the reverse. An orderly evacuation is always the quickest and leads to the minimum number of casualties. Forget your items of personal luggage. They are replaceable — you are not. Ladies should remove high-heeled shoes and sharp items of jewellery before using the evacuation slides which will be found at all exits. Fold your arms across your chest to help you on your way and ensure that they do not become damaged. Once at the bottom of the slide, leave the area as soon as possible.

Above all, in an emergency, try very hard not to panic. A cool head will get you out and in good condition. Finally, let me repeat that emergency landings are as rare as hens' teeth. Don't lose sleep worrying about them, but make sure, like all good Boy Scouts, that you are prepared.

Estimated Time of Arrival (ETA) (see also *Delays, Departure Slot, Weather*)

The estimated time of arrival is the time at which the Captain thinks the wheels will touch down, and is normally very accurate. There are two important points to bear in mind here. The ETA is not the time published in the airline schedules; any resemblance between that time and the ETA is purely coincidental! Secondly, note that I said it is the time the wheels touch down. You can add at least another 10-20min on to that time if you want to know when you will be getting off the plane. Similarly, add another 30min to 1hr if you are talking about when you will be leaving the airport. That is the time taken for customs and immigration and baggage retrieval. Clearly, if you have just been on a short domestic hop with no checked-in baggage, it will only take you a few minutes to walk out of the airport. On the other hand, if you are in the third 747 to land in as many minutes at an American airport, have lots of luggage and do not carry a US passport, then we could easily be talking 2-3hr.

The ETA will normally be announced by the Captain, either shortly before or after take-off. It will take into account the flight plan and the weather *en route* including head or tail winds. With the amount of information available to crews these days it is not surprising that the ETA is normally extremely accurate. It is rare for a flight to arrive much later than its ETA although it is not unknown for it to arrive earlier.

Explosive Decompression (see also *Oxygen Masks*)

Explosive decompression is nasty, and feared by flight and cabin crew alike. A modern airliner is, of course, pressurised so that passengers do not need oxygen masks when the aircraft is flying higher than 10,000ft. The pressure inside the fuselage is therefore greater than outside for a large portion of the flight. If the air inside the cabin is given a chance, it will rush out into the rarefied atmosphere because of the pressure difference. This is known as decompression. If the decompression happens very quickly it is known as explosive decompression. It happens when there is a serious structural failure such as a window blowing out or a door or cargo hatch breaking free.

During an explosive decompression, air is rushing out of the cabin and will continue to do so until the pressure inside and outside is the same. The outrush of air is extremely violent and will carry with it anything which is not strapped or bolted in position. It is perfectly normal for items of hand-baggage, magazines, drinks etc to fly out of windows or doors. Passengers who are not belted into their seats are likely to follow them. It is quite common for adults to be sucked through windows or the smallest hole. This is certainly one reason for obeying the Captain's request to keep seat belts fastened at all times except when moving around in the cabin. In a famous incident in 1990, the Captain of British Airways' flight 5390 was partly sucked out of the cockpit of his BAC 1-11 when a windscreen panel blew out, causing explosive decompression. The panel had apparently been re-fitted with the wrong screws after maintenance. The rest of the crew took it in turns to hold on to his legs until an emergency landing was made. Miraculously, he survived with relatively minor injuries.

The decompression is accompanied by a mist of water vapour forming in the cabin. If the aircraft is at cruising altitude, the oxygen masks will be released automatically from their overhead compartments and should be used immediately. Expect the aircraft to go into a steep dive. Do not be frightened by it — the aircraft is not out of control. The pilot is following the normal procedure, which is to get down below 10,000ft as quickly as possible. Below this altitude, oxygen is not required and the masks can be removed. Unless serious structural damage accompanies the decompression, which is rare, there is no reason why the landing should not be a normal one, although you might be told to adopt the brace position as a precaution.

Although frightening, explosive decompressions rarely result in more damage than a few shattered nerves. I hope that you never get to experience one.

Fear of Flying (see also *Alcohol, Turbulence, Weather*)

This is a problem that many people suffer from, and has been analysed at length by people far more competent than myself. It does seem to me, however, that there are three quite separate types of fear that exist. The first is fairly common and is a completely irrational phobia — a person simply hates even the thought of being in the air. There's even a word for it — pterophobia. People all over the world suffer from phobias about all kinds of things and, I'm afraid, it's simply a fact of life. I feel genuinely sorry for anyone with a phobia about flying, though, because it restricts their world so much. Other forms of transport available are boats and trains but the incredibly long journey times involved often preclude their use.

The second type of fear is the one that this book is really all about. A person can be afraid of flying because they don't understand enough about it. The bumps, whirring noises, clicks and bangs are all terrifying if you don't understand them. If you don't know about it, the noises from the undercarriage coming down and locking into position can sound awfully like a wing falling off! At different times I have known three people who were terrified in an aircraft because they thought that if the engines all failed at once it would drop like a stone. They all spent the entire flight listening to the engine noise, praying that it wouldn't stop. Every time the pilot eased back slightly on the throttles to take account of the plane's lighter weight as fuel was used up, they damn near had a heart attack. When they found out the truth, that even if all the engines did fail (and this has happened), the aircraft would be able to glide for hundreds of miles, if necessary, to find an airport to land at, their fear vanished.

Before I cover the third type of fear, a little story. Some people are exactly the opposite of those just dealt with. If they don't understand something, they simply put all their faith in the person in charge, believing (because they want to) that he or she is infallible. This goes particularly for anyone wearing a peaked hat. My mother-in-law is just like that. A few years ago, we took her with us for a holiday to Portugal. (No, you're wrong. It was a great holiday!) Anyway, it was the first time she had flown. The outbound trip was fine and without incident. Coming home, however, the weather was absolutely lousy

— gale force winds and driving rain with a cloud base lower than your kneecaps. The flight was quite bumpy, but the tension in the cabin really began to rise as we approached East Midlands Airport. The surface winds were gusting and shearing horribly as we came in for the landing. The poor pilot must have been having one hell of a time just keeping the wings level. As he tried to put the aircraft down, it was obvious that it simply didn't want to know. The seasoned flyers on board all knew that the end of the runway couldn't be far away, and there were no signs of the power being applied to come round for another try. Nervous glances between passengers said 'I'll get into the brace position if you will'. Anyway, at the last minute, the pilot elected to go for it and slammed us down on the tarmac from what must have been 20ft. All the overhead lockers were jolted open, duty-free bottles were everywhere, the oxygen masks came down and general chaos reigned. My mother-in law, who thought it was all perfectly normal, loved it!

Enough of that. The third type of fear, and one that I occasionally suffer from, is more difficult to deal with. It is a completely logical fear concerning the not-so-nice issues of the day. There have been times when I really would have preferred not to fly because of bomb-threats against the airline I intended to use. There have been other times when the air traffic controllers of a particular country have been on strike and I know full well that the system must have been dangerously overloaded. There have been yet other times when a particular engine type has just exploded somewhere in the world. The reason hasn't been found and, as I look out of the window, I see one hanging under the very wing that's keeping me in the air! Statistics don't help. We all know that flying is the safest form of travel but nevertheless a plane crash is almost always so horribly final. If you are involved in a pile-up on the M1, the chances are that you will get out in one piece. If one aircraft hits another at 35,000ft, it is a different story.

If fear of flying is a problem to you, for whatever reason, then you might like to get in touch with one of the excellent groups who run special familiarisation classes for people just like yourself. All good travel agents or the airlines themselves will be able to give you contact addresses.

First Class (see also *Bumping, Concorde, Meals*)

The sheer luxury of flying first class can only be improved on by not having to pay for it. The happiest passenger on any flight is the one who has been upgraded to first class.

The seats recline to an almost horizontal position (usually around 60°), the leg-room is enormous (seat pitch is some 60in) and they are big enough to have a party in!

As you would expect, service is superb. Most airlines work on a ratio of one cabin attendant to every four passengers. Press the service button and an attendant will be at your side almost immediately. Nothing is too much trouble. Food, drinks, blanket baths — no problem.

It's totally over the top, of course. No one this side of the intensive care ward needs that kind of attention. But people still pay the fare. I suppose that if money is absolutely no object, then you may as well have the best that's going. Ego and the ostentatious display of wealth also play their part, I'm sure.

Concorde, of course, is entirely first class and costs even more. But this I can understand. Can't afford it but can understand it. If you are in a hurry, it's the only machine on the planet that will do the job so taking it can be justified. But first class on a normal subsonic jet is a strange thing to understand. I've done it many times myself — all as a result of upgrading. I've never actually bought a first class ticket, and probably never will. Either I'm right in my view that it's a very odd experience or there's something decidedly odd about me. I hate all the attention. I like to be left alone unless I ask for something. And I like to be part of an anonymous row of seats; not stuck out on my own in the middle of the floor, as has happened several times. It's almost like being on an operating table!

My advice, then, is to leave first class to the ego-trippers. If you want to splash out on a little luxury, business class is more than enough for mere mortals.

Flaps (see also *Landings*)

The stall speed of a modern jet airliner in normal flight is usually between 150-250kts. This means that, if the airspeed is reduced below that figure, the aircraft will stall and, if near the ground, will crash. But 150-250 kts is too fast to land safely. So how do they do it? And how does it manage to get airborne at fairly low speeds during take-off? The answer lies in the flaps.

So that the aircraft can travel at speeds low enough to land safely, but does not fall out of the sky in the process, the lift generated by the wings is increased. To do this, large sections on both the leading and trailing edges of the wings are extended progressively as the aircraft gradually loses speed for landing. You will see it happen if you watch the wings during the latter part of

Leading edge flaps on a 747

Landing

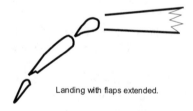

Landing with flaps extended.

TRAILING EDGE FLAPS ON A 747.

**Leading edge
flaps on a 747**

Cruising with aircraft flying "clean"

sing with aircraft flying "clean"

TRAILING EDGE FLAPS ON A 747.

the descent. You will also notice that the ride gets a little bumpier when the flaps are extended. This is because the wings are now more sensitive to small amounts of air turbulence. Noise will also be increased since the wings do not cut through the air as cleanly as they do with the flaps retracted.

Just before touchdown, when the pilot will have selected maximum flaps, the trailing edges of the wings will be pointing almost towards the ground, and daylight will be visible between the flaps and the wings. Do not panic — this is perfectly normal and does not necessarily mean that the wing is falling apart!

The aircraft will also have its flaps extended to generate extra lift during the take-off roll. This enables it to leave the tarmac at lower speeds than would otherwise be possible.

So if flaps are so incredibly efficient, why aren't they used during the entire flight? The answer is that, as well as increasing the lift of the wing, flaps also greatly increase drag. In other words, there is more resistance by the air to the plane moving forwards. Much greater amounts of fuel would therefore have to be burned, the flight would be considerably more choppy and there would be greater stress on the airframe. The pilot will therefore ensure that his aircraft is 'flying clean' as soon after take-off as possible.

Flightdeck (see also *Aircraft, Captain, Fly-By-Wire*)

Otherwise known as the cockpit. Unless the pilot is a lady.

This is where it all happens. The flightdeck is straight from the 'Boys' Own Annual' with its flashing lights, instruments, radios and more buttons than the Pearly Queen's Sunday best. Usually the home of either two or three flight crew, you may be lucky enough to be allowed on the flightdeck during a flight. It's always worth asking anyway.

The first thing you will probably notice is that no one seems to be doing anything. Visitors are normally allowed up front only during slack times, when the aircraft is on-course at cruising altitude and being flown by the automatic pilot. If the aircraft is a short-haul or one of the new computerised jobs, there will probably be two Flight Officers. If it is a wide-bodied long-haul,

Left: The flightdeck of the DC-9 series 50. Right: The Airbus A310 flightdeck. Note the computerised displays.

there will be three — The Captain, First Officer and Flight Engineer.

Thinking about it, a visit to the flightdeck will probably be a bit of a disappointment if you are over 10 years old. The flight crew tend to treat you like a moron and won't tell you anything you don't already know. If you just stand there looking impressed, they will continue with their 'pretty lights' monologue. If you start to ask intelligent questions, they will assume you are a 'smart alec' trying to catch them out and immediately clam up.

It only begins to become interesting if you have seen a few flightdecks in your time and know what you are looking for. Your first visit to a fly-by-wire flightdeck such as in the Airbus series or Boeing 747-400 aircraft should be a memorable one. The solid-state displays and computer screens give the place more the feeling of a science laboratory than a cockpit. A visit to the flight deck of Concorde is also a bit weird in that everything looks

old-fashioned these days. Because of its futuristic shape and performance, it is hard to believe that it was designed some 20 years ago!

So, by all means have a look at the flightdeck if you can arrange it. Bear with the crew — remember they have had to do all this hundreds of times before. And, most importantly, don't push any of those buttons!

The relatively simple flightdeck of the Twin Otter.

Flight Level (see also *Air Traffic Control, Altitude*)

The flight level is the altitude above sea-level at which an aircraft is flying. It is abbreviated, so that a flight level of 35,000ft is known as 350.

The idea of separate, but fixed, flight levels was dreamed up by someone in air traffic control many moons ago. In the early days of aviation, you simply flew at whatever height you felt like. Since the skies are so big, there were hardly any collisions in the air and the controllers were all a bit worried about losing their jobs. So they came up with a great idea. You bunch all the aircraft in to just a few flight levels. Now it's much easier for them to hit each other. As long as they have the same latitude and longitude, the fixed flight level will do the rest! Suddenly, overnight, air traffic controllers became worth their weight in gold! Keeping airliners out of each other's way became a highly-skilled job. Only joking, but it does make you think, doesn't it?

Flight Number (see also *Boarding Card, Check-In, Tickets, Airline Codes*)

If you forget everything else about your flight, at least memorise your flight number. It's the easiest way of knowing which aeroplane you are supposed to be on and which gate it is departing from. The destination alone is next to useless, since there will almost certainly be more than one flight to any place from any airport within a short space of time. It's slightly better if you can remember the airline as well, but the flight number has it all.

It consists of a prefix of letters identifying the airline, or carrier as it is known, followed by the number of the flight. For instance, BA denotes British Airways, CX is Cathay Pacific and so on. So BA155, for instance, would be flight code 155 operated by British Airways. As long as you know the flight number and day of departure, you will be OK.

Always check the departure screens for the latest information on your flight.

Flight Times (see also *Delays, Estimated Time of Arrival*)

This is the actual time spent in the air between take-off and landing. Obviously, it is closely related to the estimated time of arrival. The Captain will normally give out details of flight time either at the ramp or shortly after take-off. He will take into account the routeing in his flight plan, together with information he has on weather *en route* and likely congestion levels at the destination airport.

The flight time is normally very accurate, but will be different from the time given in the airline schedules, which just use a rough approximation and obviously cannot account for all the things that are happening on the day of the flight.

Fly-By-Wire (see also *Aircraft*)

Traditionally, the control surface of the aircraft (the ailerons, elevators and rudder, etc.) are connected to the yoke by either fixed metal rods or hydraulic systems. These are susceptible to damage in some circumstances and are not easily interfaced to computer control. The modern generation of airliners, therefore, uses a system known as fly-by-wire, in which the connections are electrical and can be directly controlled by an on-board computer if necessary. The pilot's yoke has been reduced from something that always dominated the cockpit to a minute device resembling a computer game joystick. In the case of the Airbus, it has even been ousted from its traditional place directly in front of the pilot and is now located to the side, much like a car's gear lever.

Coming soon, we are promised, is yet another development; that of fly-by-light. In this system, the instructions will be relayed to the control surfaces by pulses of light along optic fibres. Whatever next? My money goes on fly-by-thought!

Fuel (see also *Emergency Landings, Jettisoning Fuel*)

At take-off, a 747 on a long-haul route will have almost one half of its total weight taken up by fuel. A fully-loaded Jumbo is, quite literally, a flying fuel tank.

Jet fuel is expensive. Very expensive. It is therefore imprinted in the mind of every pilot that fuel should not be wasted. Engines will not be started until very close to the allotted time for taxying out. Flight plans will be drawn up to minimise the head winds *en route*. Autopilots will be used wherever possible, since they make far more efficient use of the engines than a human ever could. Every attempt will be made to arrive on time to minimise stacking delays over the destination airport.

The most favoured Captain of an airline these days is not likely to be the most experienced, the one with the best 'bedside manner' or even the best aviator. He will be the pilot who is the most fuel-efficient and therefore saves the airline the most money.

Yet, occasionally, fuel will be wasted. The likely result is a major inquiry by an airline. The guilty party will be found, and steps will be taken to ensure that it doesn't happen again. Loss of fuel could be caused by poor maintenance, leading to an aircraft diverting or turning back. In the latter case, large amounts of fuel may have to be dumped. It may be that a passenger becomes drunk or hostile. Perhaps weather maps were incorrectly interpreted.

Whatever the reason, the efficient use of fuel is often the dividing line between financial success and bankruptcy for an airline.

Gates (see also *Boarding Card, Departure Lounge*)

I don't know why they're called gates, because they are not really gates at all. A gate is just the name of a passenger collection area and (sometimes) lounge at that point in the airport where the aircraft departs from.

You must find out, either when you check-in or by reading the departures board, which gate your flight is departing from. Whilst waiting in the departure lounge, the time will come when you will be told that your aircraft is ready for boarding. This will be done either by an announcement over a public address system or by a message on the flight departure board, usually accompanied by flashing lights. You will, at the same time, be told the number of the gate from which your aircraft is departing. Whether you decide to get to the gate early is largely a matter of personal choice. If you like to sit down, read a book (preferably this one) and be left in peace, then it's often a good place to

G

be. But do check beforehand on the facilities provided at or near the gate area — in some airports there aren't even any seats!

Make sure that the gate you are waiting at is the right one. The flight number, destination and (often fictional) departure time will all be prominently displayed. Incidentally, it is a good idea to note the gate number shown on the departure board even if you were told it when you checked in. A lot can happen in an airport between check-in time and departure time and it is possible that your gate number could have been changed for operational reasons. Be sure that you know where your boarding card is, since you will need it to get on the aircraft.

A typical 'gate'. In this case, Number 41 at Birmingham Airport. Always double-check with the screen that you're at the right one.

The boarding procedure, particularly on a large aircraft, is normally done in stages to avoid congestion in the aisles. The first is the pre-boarding stage, when passengers with small children or other passengers needing extra time to get on to the aircraft will be allowed on board. The next stage varies from airline to airline, but it is usual to allow first class passengers to board at any stage in the process. On some airlines, this courtesy is also extended to business class passengers. Boarding of the main cabin usually takes place from the rear of the aircraft forwards, again to ensure that aisles do not become unnecessarily obstructed. The boarding call is usually made by row number and so you will need to be aware of the row number of your seat, which is printed on your boarding card. At some airports, in order to speed up boarding, it is normal to use two jetways for a wide-bodied aircraft, two adjacent departure gates therefore being used. One is used for first and business class and the other for economy passengers. If this is the case, do

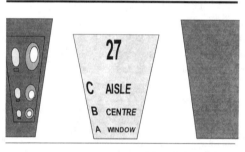

The row number and seat identification is usually written on the underside of the overhead luggage rack.

make sure that you are in the correct queue.

I find that it is best to get on board the aircraft at the earliest opportunity. The aisles are then relatively clear of other passengers, it is easier to get to your seat (particularly if you have a window or centre seat) and you will find that the overhead compartments for your hand baggage are still empty. I always try to get to the departure gate around 10 minutes before the flight is called. The departure gate itself is normally a lounge and so there will be seats available and it is often more comfortable than the departure lounge itself.

Groundspeed (see also *Airspeed, Estimated Time of Arrival*)

I'm going to amaze you all here. The groundspeed is the speed over the ground! This is not to be confused with airspeed, which can be the same as groundspeed in still air or higher or lower than groundspeed with a head wind or tail wind, respectively. The groundspeed is the important one in determining how long it is going to take to reach your destination. Sometimes, if you are lucky, a long-haul flight can reach its destination as much as an hour early. This is because it has a tail wind but flies at the same airspeed. Its groundspeed is then the airspeed plus the speed of the tail wind. Obviously, it is travelling faster over the ground than it would in still air and so it gets there quicker. Have I made myself clear?

Hand-Baggage (see also *Baggage, Carousel, Duty-Free*)

Hand-baggage is an absolute lifeline. If you are going away for only a few days, do everything in your power to make sure all your bits and bobs fit into your hand-baggage. There are several reasons for this. Firstly, the process of checking-in is faster and more straightforward. At many airports (particularly in the US) there are express check-in desks for passengers with hand-luggage only. Secondly, you have access to all your things at all times during the flight. When you are handed a landing card to complete, you won't suddenly realise that you need your passport number and your passport is in the brown suitcase in the hold! Finally, you won't have to hang around the baggage carousel like a zombie for an hour or so, only to find that your luggage didn't make it. You can walk straight from immigration through customs and out of the airport. It's wonderful!

The question on everyone's lips will be 'So how much luggage am I allowed to take on a plane?' Well, there are normally restrictions on the number of pieces, their size and their weight. Recently, however, a whole new industry has emerged which specialises in designing bags which just about get away with it, and can hold everything but the kitchen sink. The usual number restriction is one piece, although men are allowed an additional briefcase or similar. Ladies are slightly luckier, because they can also have their handbag, making a total of three pieces in all. On top of that is the bag with your duty-free in it.

The main size requirement is that your hand-baggage must fit in the over-head locker. Lots of airlines have 'dummy' lockers at either the check-in desk or the gate, so that you can try your luggage for size. The secret here is to go for soft bags, which can be pummelled into any shape you like. The current fashion appears to be for huge foldover devices that hold clothes without creasing them, but which can even be rolled up small if necessary. They also hold shoes, toiletries and anything else you might need. The science of hand-baggage manufacture is now so precise that I can live quite comfortably for a week on the contents of my hand-baggage. And yes, I do change my shirts and underwear every day!

Holidaymakers

Holidaymakers are just like company car drivers. If that thought seems a wee bit illogical, allow me to explain. If you have a company car, then you look down on all those poor devils who haven't got one because they are obviously in a much inferior job. If you haven't got one, then you look down on all those poor devils who have because they really have nothing. If they lose their job, their car goes as well.

It's just the same with holidaymakers. The business traveller — the bread and butter of the airlines' business — looks down on the holidaymaker. He sees them in the same way that a professional driver sees Sunday drivers. They are a bloody nuisance because they choke up the airports with their charter flights to Benidorm or wherever. They never know what they are doing and just amble around the airport in an apparently aimless manner, getting in the way of the serious flyer. The business flyer will also usually be flying business class, whilst virtually all the poor sods going on holiday will be back in economy. There's no doubt about it — the business traveller is a far superior being.

The holidaymaker, however, sees it in a slightly different way. He is there by choice and not because the boss has told him to get to Libya immediately or be sacked. When the holidaymaker gets to his destination, he has nothing to do for a couple of weeks but enjoy himself. The businessman, on the other hand, has to work. No, without doubt the holidaymaker is the guy on top.

They both have a point, of course, but the answer is that both types of traveller have a perfect right to be flying and neither is superior in any way to the other. The guy I hate is the one who travels frequently on business for 50 weeks of the year and then finds himself flying somewhere on holiday with the family. He does not consider himself a holidaymaker at all. He's the one at the check-in queue, making all sorts of stupid comments designed to let everyone else in the airport know he's a regular flyer. Just so you don't miss him, here are some examples.

'Of course, I never normally use the economy check-in!' 'Didn't you crew for me *en route* to Japan recently?' 'This economy experiment is a disaster. Next year, darling, we'll fly first class, the way I normally do.' And so on. Sickening isn't it?

Speaking as a regular flyer, only one thing is certain. If I had to choose between flying first class and working, or flying economy and enjoying myself, I know which I'd choose. Send me down the back of the plane and pass me the sun tan lotion!

Hot Towels

Not exactly up there with wings and engines on my 'rather important' list, but nevertheless something of a legend. Allow me to explain why. There is a set of laws called the Laws of Thermodynamics. They explain how things warm up, transfer heat and other boring things like that. There are only two things in the Universe that break those rules. The first is the warping of the space-time continuum, postulated to exist in the vicinity of black holes near the event horizon (write to Stephen Hawking for a full explanation) and the second is the hot towel. Often handed out shortly after take-off, after meals and before landing, they are presented to you in the grip of a pair of metal tongs. As you take one, your skin will suffer third-degree burns unless you immediately juggle it between your hands so that it is airborne most of the time. Then, within a split second, it is stone cold. It was at the right temperature for wiping your face and hands for around a millionth of a second. Where did all the heat go? Strange things, hot towels.

Ice (see also *Disasters, Weather*)

Ice used to be a killer in the air. Supercooled raindrops or water vapour in clouds would freeze on to aircraft, ruining the aerodynamic properties of the wings and propellers, adding weight to the airframe and clogging air intakes and carburettors. Thankfully, with modern jet aircraft, this menace has almost entirely disappeared. At the cruising altitude of a jet, the air temperature outside is a rather chilly -30°C; far too cold for ice to form. There is very little water vapour in the air at that temperature anyway. The speed of a jet also helps, since air friction on the leading-edge of the wings (the surface on which ice normally first forms) keeps them relatively warm.

There are, though, still two occasions when even a modern jet needs to take care. The first is with the runway itself. Airport authorities are always quick to melt any runway ice with either salt or one of the special de-icing compounds available these days. Even so, a pilot must always take care in sub-zero conditions.

The second problem is the de-icing procedure before take-off. Ice can form whilst the aircraft is at the terminal. If this is not cleared before take-off, the additional weight or lack of proper aerodynamic properties can cause an aborted take-off or worse. An additional problem can be the blocking of the pitot-tube, which measures the speed of the aircraft. False information from this instrument can lead to disastrous decisions in the cockpit. This is exactly what happened with Air Florida's flight 90 leaving Washington DC for Fort Lauderdale in January 1982. Although the aircraft went through the correct anti-icing procedures on the apron, the queue for take-off was so long that ice had a chance to re-form on the wings and in the pitot-tubes. The aircraft became airborne at the wrong airspeed and immediately crashed into the ice-cold Potomac River just beyond the airport boundary.

A lesson, then, that the effects of ice cannot be ignored even with today's technology, including electric heating of wing leading edges, waste water drains and water supply pipes.

Immigration (see also *Customs, Queues*)

Immigration starts whilst you are still at 35,000ft. You will be asked if you require a landing card. You usually do if the country you are about to land in is your destination but not your home country. One landing card per person is the norm, but some countries ask for one per family group. Make sure that you fill in these forms in full.

Immigration queues are legendary for their length and slowness. Try any trick you can to get to the front. If the aircraft is using a jetway to disembark, be first off the plane. If, however, it is parked in the middle of the apron and buses are being used to ferry passengers to the terminal, be the last one on to

On arrival, simply follow the directions to Passport Control.

Make sure that you get into the right queue at Immigration.

the first bus. You'll be first off!

The immigration officer will ask you a set of questions which are almost always the same. What is the purpose of your visit? What is your occupation? Where will you be staying? When will you be leaving the country? Never try to joke with these people. Give your occupation as 'Spy' and you will be in jail for 48hr. You'll also cause massive delays to everyone behind you, so no one's going to feel like putting in a good word on your behalf. If you don't know where you will be staying, don't say so. Use the address of your Embassy, or give the name of the hotel where you would like to stay.

Good luck and be patient!

In-Flight Entertainment (see also *Airshow, Alcohol, Seats, Sleeping*)

The worst part about any flight, especially the long-haul ones, is the terrible, soul-destroying, inescapable boredom of it all. There you are, sitting in your seat next to a perfect stranger. You know that nothing is going to change for the next eight hours or so. What are you going to do to retain your sanity?

Different people approach the problem in different ways. Some people get themselves engrossed in a book. An increasing number of passengers, particularly the younger ones, bring their Walkman along and listen to their favourite music. It's a totally new sound of the latter part of the 20th century, you know. That horrible, jingly, tinny sound of someone else's Walkman. Loud enough so that you can't ignore it but impossible to decipher what they're listening to. Forget the segregation of smokers. The question ought to be 'Walkman or Non-Walkman, sir?' A soundproof wall should divide the two.

Others try to engage their neighbour in conversation. Frankly, I'd rather have a Walkman sitting next to me. The chances are that I've absolutely nothing in common with the person in the next seat. After the flight, I'll probably never see

85

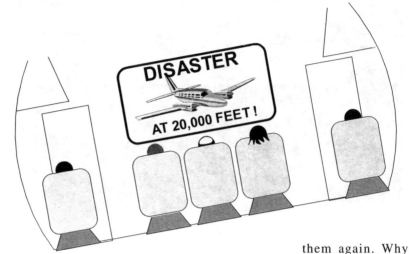

Forget No Smoking -
No Walkmen would
be a better idea!

them again. Why try like mad to find something to talk about? If you are like me, the best thing to do is learn the word for 'pardon me?' in a couple of foreign languages and assume a vacant expression if they try to make contact. Be careful, though. Once you have started this charade, there's no turning back. You can't speak to him in Swahili one minute and then to the cabin attendant in a Cambridge accent the next. One way round it is to use a very slow pidgin English to the stewardess. Just

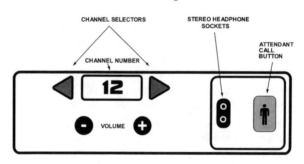

A TYPICAL SEAT CONSOLE

SATELLITE TV'S GREAT FOR THE PASSENGERS BUT IT DOESN'T HALF ADD TO THE DRAG !

enough grammar for her
to understand what you want but not
enough for you to sound English. Try it — it can be fun!

Another alternative, and the one that I have come to favour over the years, is to sleep. It is the quickest way to pass the time, it stops the unwanted conversations and you generally arrive feeling nicely refreshed. Be sure that you leave instructions with the steward or stewardess on when you want to be woken. You may not want to miss meals or the duty-free sales.

Since I am deliberately omitting any mention of the mile-high club (write in for details of the secret membership sign), the final way to pass time on a flight is to make use of the in-flight entertainment provided in the form of audio tapes and film videos. As far as the audio side is concerned, the Hawkins Laws of Certainty apply. These are as follows- 1) You will read the tape listings in the in-flight magazine and find only one track that you want to hear; 2) When you start listening to the tape, you will begin at the track after the one that you wanted to hear; 3) You will then forget about it all for some time until it occurs to you to have a listen again; 4)

GAME BOYS BREAK THE MONOTONY - BUT THEY DON'T HALF MAKE YOUR ARMS ACHE !

See 2) above; 5) This time, you decide not to let yourself forget. You listen to all the rubbish on the rest of the tape, just to make sure you don't miss your track; 6) Just as it is about to play, either- a) the stewardess will want to know what you want for dinner, or b) the Captain will begin a 30-minute-long address over the intercom, telling you that you are now flying over the ancient city of Glod, but you can't see it because the cloud cover is total; 7) In a fit of ultra-frustration, you eat the headphones.

If you really must listen to the audio entertainment, you will find that flying with an airline whose nationality is the same as your own helps a lot. The biggest differences between people of different countries are their sense of humour and tastes in music. If you find that hard to believe, just cast your mind back to the Eurovision Song Contest!

The highlight of most people's flight is the film (or films if you are on a really long haul). I can't think why. The picture quality is dreadful. The sound is worse. There's always a Texan wearing the world's largest stetson in the

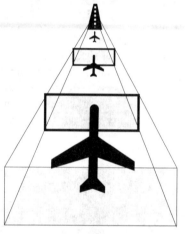

Landing by Instruments-
A Plane's view of the glideslope

row in front of you. It is either the middle of the night and you can't keep your eyes open or there is bright sunshine outside and some fool near the screen wants to keep his blind up so that he can watch the clouds go by. Needless to say, the patch of light from his window obscures all the action. They also have a nasty habit of breaking down. Some time ago I saw *Indiana Jones and The Last Crusade en route* to the States. It was 10 minutes from the end. They had just drunk from the chalice. Would it bring everlasting

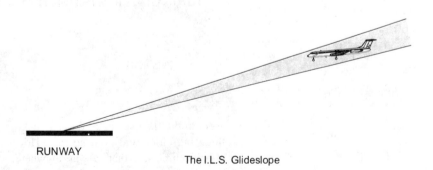

RUNWAY

The I.L.S. Glideslope

life or instant death? We never found out. The blasted tape broke. Hundreds of people promptly charged into Dallas Fort Worth Airport, stopping total strangers and threatening to strangle them if they didn't describe the end of the film.

The latest development in in-flight entertainment is the personal video fitted into the seat-back. Now this might sound like a good idea. At least it gets rid of the problem of the man with the big hat! The trouble is that you need eyes like a hawk to see the screen. It's hard enough to make out the actors, even when you have 20/20 vision. If you want to read the credits, you'll need a telescope big enough to read Neil Armstrong's name badge!

Oh well, that's entertainment!

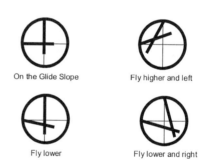

On the Glide Slope

Fly higher and left

Fly lower

Fly lower and right

INSTRUCTIONS TO PILOT DURING AN INSTRUMENT LANDING

Instrument Landings (see also *Automatic Pilot*)

I used to worry myself sick when we were in the final stages of descent and a look out of the window revealed nothing but cloud and pouring rain. How could the pilot land in this? How could he even be sure that he was anywhere near the runway? Nine times out of 10, the plane popped out of the cloud at

89

around 1,000ft, we were in exactly the right place and the landing was normal. Then, one day, it didn't. I didn't even realise what had happened at the time. We were getting lower and lower — that much I could sense. Then we seemed to stop descending, the engines began roaring but the ride was much smoother. While I was still trying to figure out what was happening, sweating all the while, a message came over the public address system from the pilot. We were told that we had just made a full instrument landing! We were, in fact, happily taxying to our gate and I still couldn't see anything outside!

Since that time, I have never been worried by any weather conditions during landing. Coming in on instruments is, if anything, smoother than the manual equivalent. Sailing in down a radar corridor is a precise science. So stop worrying.

The three autopilots connected to the instrument landing system carry out the instrument landing. The localiser on the ground sends out a precise beam to mark the glide slope. The autopilots centre the aircraft on the localiser beam and keep it there all the way down to the runway.

Don't look out of the window if the lack of view upsets you. Read this book instead — and don't panic!

International Date Line (see also *Time Differences*)

The International Date Line confuses more people than any other subject, with the possible exception of what happened to The Osmonds. How is it possible that, on one side of a line it is Saturday, whilst on the other it is still Friday?

I will attempt to make everything crystal clear, dear reader. The first crucial

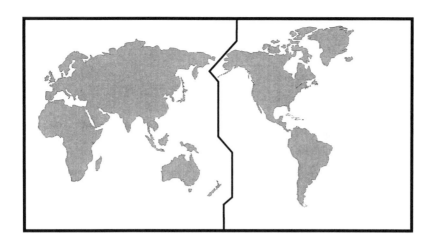

The International Date Line (180 degrees)

step is to realise that the day doesn't really change at all. The time change across the Date Line is just as smooth as anywhere else on Earth. The Date Line meanders its way from the North to South Poles, bobbing and weaving to avoid slicing islands in two and creating terrible chaos amongst natives who wouldn't even know what day it was! It has a longitude of 180°, which means it is directly opposite the Greenwich meridian which has a longitude of 0°. So when it is midday in Greenwich, it is midnight on the Date Line. On the eastern side of the line, it is after midnight. On the western side it is not yet midnight and therefore a day earlier. I shall be testing you on all this later so pay attention.

Why bother with a Date Line at all? Well, if we didn't, we'd all be able to share in the secrets of eternal youth and that wouldn't do at all would it? Geriatrics would be an obsolete profession for a start, and just think of the size of the European Phyllosan mountain. The reason is that if we spent some time whizzing around the Earth travelling westwards, every time we made a complete circuit we would gain a day. If we made the circuit in less than 24 hours (and this is now possible), we would be younger than when we set out. Anyone with a death wish would go like a bat out of hell in the opposite direction!

In order to keep us in line, and make sure that everyone knows which are today's newspapers, the International Date Line was put in place. If you travel westwards, you lose a day to make up for the time you have gained. Hence the expression 'a day goes west'. If you travel eastwards, you gain a day to compensate for the time lost during travel.

Easy isn't it? Now for that test...

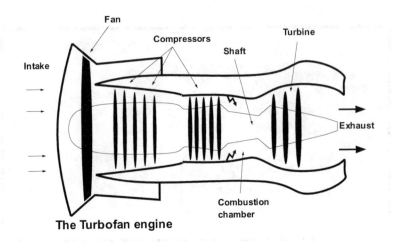

The Turbofan engine

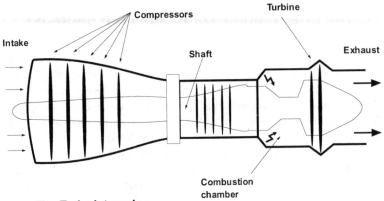

The Turbojet engine

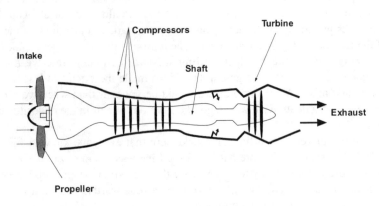

The Turboprop engine

Jet Engines (see also *Airspeed*)

Pretty useful things these — unless you happen to be a glider pilot! The engines on an aircraft provide the propulsion that gives it airspeed. It is the airspeed that keeps it flying. As an aside, it is amazing the number of people that genuinely believe that if all of the engines on an aircraft stopped suddenly in mid-flight, the aircraft would plummet to earth like a stone. It isn't true of course. If this were to happen, the nose of the aircraft would drop, thus increasing its speed until lift developed. The aircraft would then come down at a shallow angle, known as its 'glide angle'. When near the ground, the pilot can 'round out' and make a perfectly respectable attempt at a landing. Aircraft have landed safely under these conditions many times. It can be a little unnerving for the passengers, however, because the descent is quite a lot steeper than normal.

Anyway, back to engines. The biggest single advance in civil aviation was undoubtedly the jet engine. In the days before jets, all aircraft were driven along by piston engines powering propellers. Although they work, of course, there are many significant drawbacks to this type of engine. They are relatively slow, and so intercontinental journeys used to take days rather than hours; they are noisy which leads to fatigue and even deafness and they cannot fly high enough to avoid bad weather. They are, therefore, pretty uncomfortable things to be in for all but the shortest of journeys. The jet engine changed everything. Suddenly, aircraft could cruise at speeds in excess of 500kts and even supersonically. Jet engines are actually more efficient in the rarefied high atmosphere, meaning that airliners could travel above the clouds, where the air is usually quite calm and the weather always sunny. Although noisier from the ground, jet engined aircraft are quite quiet inside and it is always possible to get some sleep if you need to. The modern airliner, even the subsonic ones,

The Comet — the first commercial jet airliner.

can get you anywhere in the world within 24 hours.

The introduction of jet engines was not, however, without its problems. Pilots took some time to adjust to the fact that throttle control is not instantaneous as it is with a propeller engine. A jet engine takes a few seconds to respond. If you have got used to cooking with gas and then switched to electricity, you will know what I am talking about! The other problem is that jet engines, when the throttle is closed, do not present the drag that a propeller does and so there is no tendency to slow the aircraft. Before reverse thrust was added, aircraft would hurtle off the end of the runway!

The principle on which a jet engine is based is beautifully simple. Air mixed with fuel is compressed in a combustion chamber and ignited. It expands and is exhausted through the back of the engine, producing the thrust and propelling the engine forward. In the turbofan engine, some of the exhaust gases are used to drive a turbine. This is similar to a fan, in turn driving the compressor turbine in the combustion chamber and the intake turbine which feeds more air to the combustion chamber. In modern (high bypass ratio) jet engines, a large proportion of the incoming air bypasses the combustion chamber, producing more power and quieter operation. In the turbo-jet (the original type of jet engine), the intake turbine is omitted. The third derivative is the turbo-prop, in which the jet engine power is used to drive a propeller. This type of engine is more efficient at lower altitudes and so tends to be used on aircraft designed for short flights.

The jet age did, however, get off to something of a false start. The first commercial jet airliner was the Comet in 1953. Initially, it was plagued by a series of crashes. Some were due to metal fatigue in the airframe and some were due to the inexperience of pilots with the new type of engine. The jet engine is slower to respond to throttle changes than the propeller engine.

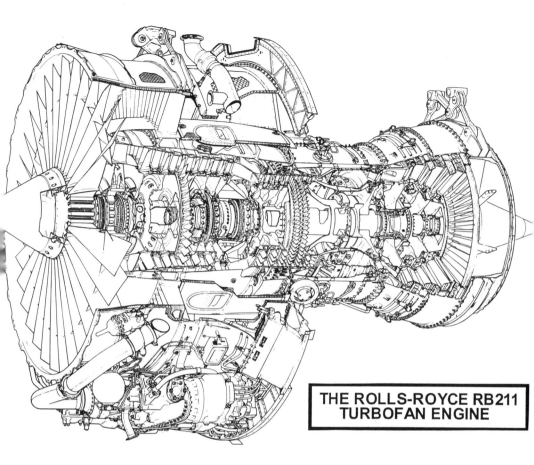

THE ROLLS-ROYCE RB211 TURBOFAN ENGINE

Idling propellers are excellent brakes on the ground, but suddenly there were none and several overshooting accidents resulted.

On the positive side, engine reliability improved dramatically. There are no plugs to foul up in a jet

engine. The rotating parts are less prone to failure than the many reciprocating (those that move backwards and forwards to you) parts on a propeller engine. This also reduces vibration, which can lead to wear. The absence of a carburettor in a jet instantly removes the problem of them icing over and stopping the engine in flight. Many other problems virtually disappeared as well. Jet engines are more efficient the higher they fly. At the normal cruising altitudes of 30,000-35,000ft, the outside air is too cold for ice to form. Even at lower altitudes, the high speed of a modern jet produces heating of the leading edges of the wings by friction, greatly reducing the chance of ice formation.

The passenger has benefited greatly from the jet engine. We now fly much faster, more quietly and at heights that are above the horrible weather conditions that older propeller aircraft had to fly through. Let your first drink on board be a toast to Sir Frank Whittle!

There are a number of manufacturers and consortia that produce jet engines for aircraft. For many years the principal players were Rolls-Royce and Pratt and Whitney, with General Electric on the sidelines. On the whole, modern jet engines have proved to be extremely reliable. Occasionally, a spate of incidents involving a particular engine type will occur, forcing a detailed look at that engine. This happened with the JT8/D after an apparent problem with the combustion chamber. Apart from isolated incidents such as these, in-flight engine failures are extremely rare. Typical rates are one shutdown for every 35 million hours — an astonishingly low failure rate. If my car were that good, I'd be a happy man! Jet engines are now considered so reliable that it is standard practice to make transatlantic crossings in 'the big twins'; wide-bodied airliners with only two engines.

Incidentally, have you ever counted the number of engines on the aircraft you are about to fly in? Try it next time and you might well be surprised. It is not uncommon for an extra engine to be found, nestling in a pod close to the fuselage under the left wing. This extra engine is simply being transported from one place to another, and this is the most economic way to do it. The Captain will adjust the trim of the aircraft to compensate for it and, after that, it will make absolutely no difference to your flight.

Jet-Lag (see also *Alcohol, Time Differences*)

Those who have never suffered from it think that jet-lag is simply your body clock being out of synchronisation with the clock on the wall. That, believe me, is doing it a great injustice. When you have jet-lag — real jet-lag — you want to die. You are sick, weak and totally disoriented. It's like the worst hangover you've ever had, multiplied a thousandfold.

Of course, the body clock error is all part of it. I've had it every way possible. I've wanted to go to bed for the night at 3 pm; I've wanted to have breakfast and start work at 3 am and I've lain in bed at the same time, wide awake, trying to convince my brain to sleep. Believe me, they're all as bad as each other.

Over the years, I've found ways to at least minimise the effects of jet-lag, if not totally eliminate it. Here is my four point plan:

1) Try to adjust yourself to the time of your destination gradually, starting two days before your journey. It won't be nearly as traumatic, doing it in your own house. Be prepared for all the neighbours and friends thinking that you've gone round the twist when you go to bed at 6 pm or have breakfast on the patio at 1 o'clock in the morning!

2) Keep to your destination time as much as you can when you are on the plane. When an attendant offers you dinner, look alarmed and say 'What, at this time in the morning?'

3) Stay away from alcoholic drinks as much as you can. They make things a lot worse.

4) Pay absolutely no attention at all to whether it is sunny or dark outside the aircraft. It's all a mirage!

If you decide to pay no attention to any of this, and arrive feeling like a reject from the sewage works, then at least try to acclimatise yourself to local time as quickly as you can. Nocturnal habits are just as weird in a foreign country!

Jettisoning Fuel (see also *Emergency Landings*)

If there is a problem with your aircraft immediately after take-off, and the problem is serious enough to mean that you have to return to the airport, the chances are that you will have to spend some time in the air dumping fuel. The reason is that a fully-fuelled Jumbo is simply too heavy to land.

The aircraft will fly to a designated area and jettison fuel, often flying in circles, until the correct landing weight has been achieved. This usually takes some time, and it is normal for a couple of hours to have passed before the wheels hit the tarmac again.

Jumbo Jet (see also *Aircraft*)

Officially, the Jumbo Jet is the nickname for the Boeing 747. It has, however, been applied to wide-bodied aircraft generally and so can include planes such as the Lockheed L1011 TriStar and the McDonnell-Douglas DC-10.

Landings (see also *Instrument Landings*)

I have sat through an awful lot of descents. They seem so often to terrify my fellow passengers. I really do not know why this should be, and the people that I have asked can never identify any single thing that upsets them. It is certainly true that, during this stage of the flight, there are a lot of things happening, some of which make strange noises which can be unnerving to the inexperienced. So let's go through a typical descent and landing procedure.

You are trundling along at cruising altitude, probably 30-40min away from the latest ETA (estimated time of arrival). The first thing you will notice is a reduction in engine noise as the pilot reduces the throttle settings for descent. The nose will drop slightly as the aircraft begins to lose height. This change in altitude is barely perceptible, but you may be able to notice it if you have a window seat and can see the horizon. The next thing that happens should be the illumination of the seat belt sign, followed by an announcement that the descent has begun and passengers should return to their seats. As the aircraft continues to lose height, it will gradually reach the level of the cloud tops, when some minor turbulence may be encountered. The flaps will be gradually extended to increase lift at low speeds and prevent the aircraft stalling as speed is reduced for landing. If you can see the trailing edge of the wing from your seat, you will notice the flaps being progressively extended during the descent. In addition to increasing lift, the flaps increase drag and some additional noise may be heard. The aircraft will be flying at low altitudes now, and so some buffeting is perfectly normal. You will hear the engines making frequent changes in pitch as adjustments are made to the throttle settings to keep the aircraft on the correct approach. As you near the airport, the landing gear will be extended. You will hear the whining of the hydraulics, followed by thumps as the wheels are locked into position. The landing gear will now be providing even greater levels of drag and so air noise will increase even more. It is quite possible that local pockets of rising or sinking air near ground level will make it necessary for the pilot to make constant minor adjustments to the flight control to keep the wings level.

The Captain will then instruct the cabin crew to take their seats and he will turn the plane on to its final approach for landing.

The nervous passenger will already have suffered more than a little tension during the descent. His pulse rate will still stay high for a few seconds yet.

Many people find the final approach to be the most uncomfortable part of the flight. The view of the ground outside is more upsetting to some passengers than is the sight of clouds below. The feel of height is more real. Anyone who is worried by heights is more likely to feel nervous when just a few hundred feet above the ground than when 35,000ft up.

Several other factors also come into play. When viewed from the airport, the approach of a plane to the runway looks like a smooth, silent and graceful affair. From inside the aircraft, however, it appears very different. There will be a lot of wind noise and buffeting caused by additional drag on the lowered undercarriage and extended flaps. The noise from the engines will vary continuously, as the pilot or automatic pilot adjusts settings to stay at the right speed and on the glide slope. In a manual approach, the pilot will be using special

A Cathay Pacific 747 on its final hair-raising approach to Hong Kong.

runway lighting techniques to stay on the glide path. When in the correct position, the approach lights will appear to be streaming past the aircraft in a symmetric way on either side. He will also be watching the transverse lights, which act as a sort of artificial horizon, telling him whether the wings are straight. His height in relation to the glide path will be shown by the Visual Approach Slope Indicators, mounted on either side of the runway. Ground-effect will cause some turbulence and so the wings will have to be brought to the level position time and time again. Then, just as the runway appears below the aircraft, the throttles will be closed as the aircraft 'flares' or raises its nose, to bleed off airspeed. All this is perfectly normal as the aircraft approaches the runway.

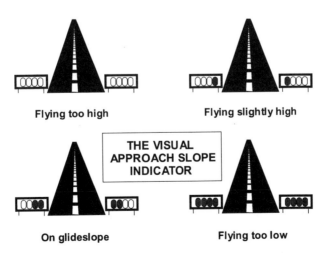

After the throttles have been closed, the aircraft seems to hover over the runway for an age. Its nose will be high at this stage. Then a little bump is felt and a slight squeal is heard on one side of the main undercarriage as it meets the ground. Often, the other side makes contact a split-second later, when there will be a second bump and squeal. It's not over yet, though. The plane will stay nose-high for several seconds as its speed decreases and the nose drops to allow the nosewheels down on to the runway. Then be prepared. Almost immediately, there will be a loud roar as reverse thrust is selected to help slow the plane down. The length of time

Electronic indicators show the pilot when he is lined up for the jetway at the ramp.

that reverse thrust is operating will depend on the weight of the aircraft and the length of the runway, especially between the landing point and the taxiway to be used. Sometimes it is not used at all.

The aircraft will now have slowed down to taxying speed, and will now commence its journey to the apron. On arrival at the gate, he will be directed to the correct position for the jetway either by ground staff or by an automatic indicator.

I could not leave a section on landing without saying something about my favourite approach in the whole world. The approach into Hong Kong from the west has to be experienced to be believed. Get yourself a window seat on the right-hand side of the aircraft, sit back and be amazed! During the very final stages of the descent, the aircraft will be flying ridiculously low over the Kowloon peninsula. You can look straight out of the window and see the locals eating their dinners in their high-rise blocks. Just when you think you are going to land in the street, there will be a sharp right-hand turn over the Walled City. Before you even have time to be terrified, your wheels will be on the tarmac of Kai Tak Airport. Don't miss it!

Latest Check-In Time (see also *Check-In, Departure Time*)

Latest check-in time is a very strange thing. Before I tell you why, I'll tell you what it is. It is the latest time you can check-in at, before your seats are given to the poor devils on the standby list. Check-in after this time, therefore, and you might not have anywhere to sit. When I tell you that they don't allow standing passengers, you'll begin to realise the enormity of the problem. It's always a good idea, therefore, to make sure that you know what your latest check-in time is. You'll find it printed on your itinerary.

Now for the strange thing. The latest check-in time never alters, no matter how long the flight is delayed. I remember one time, when my check-in time was two days before my flight finally clawed its way into the skies! Do not, therefore, make the mistake of thinking that, because your flight is delayed and everyone knows about it, you can check-in late. You can't. Them's the rules.

Lifejackets (see also *Emergency Evacuations*)

I love to watch the safety drill when they get to the bit involving lifejackets. Your lifejacket is stored under your seat. Retrieve it and remove it from its container. Place it over your head, pass the ties around the waist, bring them together at your side and then fasten them in a double bow. When outside the aircraft, pull the cord to inflate. If it fails to inflate, a tube is supplied to inflate it by blowing into it. A whistle is provided for attracting attention.

Now imagine the real thing. You are hurtling towards the sea. You may be on fire. Everyone is screaming, panicking and holding their seats and loved ones in a vice-like grip. How many people are going to remember to look under their seat?

Right. You've crashed in the sea. Water is pouring in through gashes in the fuselage. The shout goes up 'Get your lifejackets'. Half of the seats have collapsed during the impact. That's half the lifejackets gone. The lucky ones manage to get them out from under the seat. They've never seen a lifejacket before. The aircraft is sinking quickly now, as water pours in through the doors

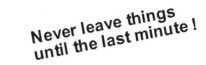

Never leave things until the last minute !

which have been opened to allow evacuation. Half the passengers get them over their heads the wrong way round, with the tube and whistle at the back. The rest have suddenly gone a blank on how to tie a double bow at the side! Several passengers just put them over their heads and pulled the cord. Now they can't tie them up. They wander through the aisles, now choked with duty-free, hand-baggage and nervous wrecks, like so many barrage balloons.

Some, however, have made it. Probably all ex-Boy Scouts, they have tied double bows that Akela would have been proud of. They jump into a 15ft swell close to freezing point. The cord is pulled. Nothing. Who is going to have the energy to blow the damn thing up by lung pressure? Even if some superhuman passenger manages to do this much, is he still going to have enough puff left to blow his whistle? He's going to be lucky if he can still manage to breathe!

I just hope that I never crash into the sea. I can't swim anyway!

Lost Property (see also *Baggage, Carousel*)

Lost property falls into one of three general headings: things that you leave in airports, things that you leave in aircraft and lost checked-in baggage.

The first two are your own fault and nobody will ever admit responsibility for the third!

Airports almost always have lost property desks where items can be reclaimed. For security reasons, however, bags left unattended will almost certainly have been searched. There has also been the odd occasion when a suspicious-looking piece of unattended baggage has been blown up in a controlled explosion!

Over the years, I have foolishly left a number of items in the overhead lockers of aircraft. The odd coat, bag of duty-free and even a camera have been forgotten in my haste to get into the immigration queue. Despite making enquiries with the airlines involved, as well as the airports themselves, I have never had a single item returned. The lesson is now learned. I always check and double-check the overhead lockers, under my seat and the seat in front and the seat pocket in front of me before leaving the aircraft. I suggest that you do the same.

If your worst nightmare comes true and the last case has been taken off the carousel while you are still bagless, do not despair. Near the carousel will be the handling agents' desks and it is to them that you must now trot. The desks will usually be marked to let you know who handles which airline's luggage. You will need your baggage receipt, which will be fixed to your ticket folder. The computer tracing system that almost all airlines use these days should find your baggage and get it to you within a few hours. So don't despair — think how nice it will be going through customs with only hand-baggage! If, by some accident, your cases are missing for more than 24hr, you may be entitled to make a claim for compensation. Bear it in mind.

A very strange thing once happened to my luggage. I arrived back in Gatwick after a trip to the States. My luggage didn't. Anyone who has gone through the experience will tell you how soul-destroying it is to wait while all the bags are unloaded on to the carousel from a packed 747. It takes for ever. As it goes on, you first get a feeling in the pit of your stomach that something is wrong. You look round. Only a handful of people are waiting now. They all look as nervous as you. One by one, they collect their bags and leave. The cases are trickling through, one every minute or so. There's only you and one other passenger left now. After an age, a bag appears through the curtain. It's his. How long do you wait to see if yours is going to appear? After all, someone is bound to be last! Then the red flashing light goes out and your flight number disappears from the screen. That's it. You've had it. Well, off I trotted to the desk. And there were my bags! They'd never been on the carousel in the first place. Apparently, because I had checked-in rather early for my flight, my bags had been put on a cargo plane leaving before my flight. They had actually arrived before I did and had been waiting there for me the whole time! So, dear passenger, if like me you tend to check-in early for flights and your cases are late off the carousel, check with the desk before abandoning all hope.

Lounges (see also *Business Class, Concorde, First Class*)

Airline lounges are a subject that you won't know or care anything about unless you travel on business or have pots of money. The reason for this is that they are reserved for use by first class (and occasionally business class) passengers. Some lounges are not operated by airlines but require you to join an 'executive club' to get in.

So what exactly are they? Well, as the name suggests, they are special lounges where you can wait for your flight in peace and quiet, away from the crowds and little Johnny who is about to pour coke down the neck of your nice new business suit. They normally offer free drinks and snacks, reading material, telephone and fax facilities (at a price) and nice comfortable seating. There is often a television to watch.

Whether or not a lounge is worthwhile depends on which airport you are flying from and the time of year. The departure lounge at Gatwick South Terminal, for instance, is hell in summer and you would be well advised to use a lounge if you have access to one (although you can always escape to the Satellite). On the other hand, it is often more pleasant to have a look round the shops or watch the aircraft movements on the apron. You pays your money and you takes your choice.

There is one little niggle that I have with lounges. When you go in, the receptionist takes your flight details so that they can inform you when your

M

flight is ready to board. All very nice. Now they think they are doing you a favour by waiting until the last minute to ask you to board. The theory that they have is that by the time you get to the gate, the queues will have gone and boarding will be less painful. This is often the case. But the one thing that has been forgotten in the middle of all this is that it is absolutely guaranteed that, by the time you find your seat, there will be nowhere to put your carry-on luggage. You won't even be able to get a toothpick in those overhead lockers! It is always a good idea, therefore, to go to the gate before you are called in the lounge and queue like everyone else. No one likes queuing, but at least you will be able to get to your 'essentials' during the flight.

Meals (see also *Alcohol, First Class, Seats*)

The subject of a book in itself! I've probably had more meals in aircraft than in restaurants and I can tell you they can be anything from exceptionally good to the most disgusting goo you have ever seen.

If you travel an airline of the Western World, then you will, at least, be able to recognise what you are eating. The quality of food and service will depend on your class of travel and length of flight. First class long-haul flight passengers will get a four/five course meal with choice of main course, served on china tableware with metal cutlery, each course being served separately as it would in a restaurant. Economy class short-haul passengers will usually get a cup of tea and a biscuit. In between these two extremes, every level of cuisine that you can think of is represented.

Flying to the Med on a charter

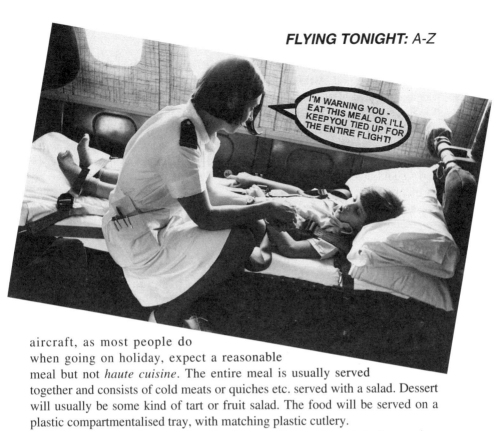

aircraft, as most people do
when going on holiday, expect a reasonable
meal but not *haute cuisine*. The entire meal is usually served
together and consists of cold meats or quiches etc. served with a salad. Dessert
will usually be some kind of tart or fruit salad. The food will be served on a
plastic compartmentalised tray, with matching plastic cutlery.

Flying economy class on a long-haul, you will normally get similar service,
but with a hot main course. Many airlines now give a choice for the entrée.

First class and, to a certain extent, business class meals always seem to be a
bit over-the-top to me. After all, the one thing that we passengers have in
common is that we are trying to get from one place to another. If we had
wanted a gourmet meal, we would have stayed where we were and visited a
restaurant. Airlines seem to be convinced that the more complicated the meal,
the better the service. Expect sautéed veal, stuffed quail, roasted guinea-hen,
lobster fricassee and the like. I yearn for steak and kidney pudding, fish and
chips, roast beef and Yorkshire pudding. You know — real food.

The problems only seem to crop up when flying an exotic airline, whose
country of origin has very different culinary habits from your own. Aeroflot
meals are a legend in their own lunchtime, but few travellers come up against
these culinary versions of a road traffic accident too often. The food served on
Far Eastern airlines can be — well — different. Trying to eat fried rice —
grain by grain — with what look like oversized toothpicks at 35,000ft is one
of life's little experiences that should not be missed.

Many airlines go absolutely overboard in their promotion of food, simply
because it is one of the few areas where airlines can get one over on each
other. Some have visiting French chefs, others feature cuisine from all over

M

the world. Believe me, you can't taste the difference. Perhaps that's a result of the cooking method. Airline food all has to be cooked around 24hr before it is eaten. It is then blast-cooled until the plane is ready to leave. On board, the food is simply re-heated in convector ovens by the cabin attendants before serving. This process rules out any type of food which does not re-heat well. You will never see a butter or egg-based sauce, since it would be curdled under a skin half an inch thick! My desire for fish and chips will never be satisfied because you simply can't re-heat deep fried food.

Incidentally, if you need a special diet for health, religious or any other reason, virtually every airline can cater for you, provided that you give them some notice. Vegetarian dishes are carried as a matter of routine. *Bon appetit.*

Military Aircraft (see also *Air Traffic Control*)

It's amazing how often you can catch a glimpse of military aircraft, particularly fighters, when you are ambling through the sky, eating your dinner and minding your own business.

You won't see them for long, however. They love to show-off to the civil pilots by doing their 'Top Gun' thing. I suppose it must be a bit like the boy-racer in the Ferrari at the traffic lights, proving that he can out-drag you in your Volvo!

They will always be some considerable distance away, as Tornado pilots and the like are not, thank goodness, immune from the clutches of air traffic control. It does brighten up an otherwise dull flight to see one of these boys charging past you with his backside on fire, making you think you've stopped when you're really doing over 500 miles an hour!

"Christ - he's moving !"
"So would you if your bum was on fire !"

Navigation (see also *Air Traffic Control, Automatic Pilot, Instrument Landings*)

Have you ever wondered, sitting there in the blue, with a blanket of uninterrupted white cloud below, how the pilot can ever manage to find a small strip of tarmac that is at the moment several thousand miles away? The answer, you will be pleased to know, is not just guess-work.

In the early days of flight, navigation was by 'dead-reckoning'. You simply plotted the bearing for your destination, corrected it a little bit for wind speed and direction, and there you were — lost! Pinpointing ground features

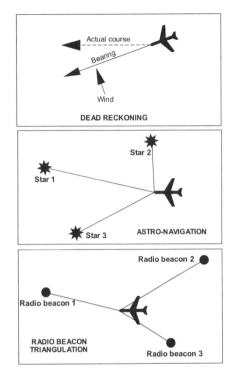

EARLY NAVIGATION METHODS

or taking bearings on stars helped correct the drift, but the whole thing was very hit-or-miss. Things improved a little when Morse code radio was installed, but its limited range of a hundred miles or so wasn't much use to pilots way off course. Things were better when three radio stations could be contacted at the same time, and a bearing taken from each one. The process known as triangulation could then be used to obtain an accurate position. When radio range increased, the crew could stay in radio contact for at least most of a flight, helping matters considerably.

Then came radar. In addition to maps of the terrain below, radar could be used to help fix position by measuring the delay in arrival between two signals from two different transmitters. Radio lanes soon became available over land, the pilots knowing when they passed directly over a radio beacon. Doppler radar came next, providing much more useful information, including the drift of the aircraft due to wind and its groundspeed.

Then came a revolution. Probably the greatest invention in navigation since the sextant — the inertial navigation systems (INS) fitted to all modern aircraft enable the crew to know exactly where they are on the globe at any time. And like most good inventions, it is basically a very simple device.

The INS is based on the gyroscope. As any schoolchild knows, once a

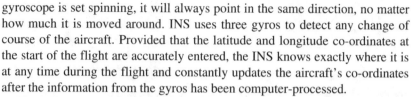

gyroscope is set spinning, it will always point in the same direction, no matter how much it is moved around. INS uses three gyros to detect any change of course of the aircraft. Provided that the latitude and longitude co-ordinates at the start of the flight are accurately entered, the INS knows exactly where it is at any time during the flight and constantly updates the aircraft's co-ordinates after the information from the gyros has been computer-processed.

The INS is also connected to the automatic pilot. Since way-points and turning points are also loaded into the INS, the autopilot flies the plane according to the flight plan without any human intervention.

The weakness of the system is the one part where human input is required. The starting point co-ordinates must be accurately entered and the aircraft must then remain stationary until the gyro platform has stabilised. If the wrong co-ordinates are stored, or the aircraft is moved too soon, the INS will provide false information. It is now thought that the Korean Airlines flight KAL 007 that was shot down in Soviet airspace was a victim of erroneous readings from the INS after the aircraft was moved too soon after entering the location data.

Night Flights (see also *Jet-Lag, Sleeping*)

I've always hated night flights. Everything seems to be wrong with them. First of all, there's all the hassle of getting to the airport and checking-in when your brain is telling you that you should have been in bed several hours ago. Then there's the flight itself. All you want to do is sleep, but the attendants are failing in their duty if they don't keep asking you what you want to drink, or read, or eat or whatever. Then there's the arrival. Unless the flight is a really long one, you arrive at some ridiculous hour in the morning, when every self-respecting taxi driver is still in his bed and buses are rarer than truthful politicians.

You finally make it to the hotel, absolutely shattered. If you are on holiday, you now have the choice of either forcing yourself to enjoy it or catching up on your sleep and missing a day of your holiday. If you are travelling on business, a new working day is just starting and you're off to a meeting where you need to be alert and wide awake. It's a disaster.

It has nothing to do with the airline, you know. Don't believe those advertisements that tell you that if you fly FredAir or whoever, you will arrive totally refreshed and relaxed. Absolute rubbish. You've missed a proper night's sleep, whoever you fly with.

I always try to get daytime flights, aiming to arrive at the destination airport in time to get to your final destination at around 6-7 pm local time. That gives you time to change, have a drink, have dinner and then off to bed at a reasonable time. Not too early and not too late.

Next morning you will be bright-eyed and bushy-tailed. Well, it works for me!

Oxygen Masks (see also *Altitude, Emergency Landings, Explosive Decompression*)

The cabin of a jet aircraft is pressurised to allow the passengers to breathe normally. This is necessary because, above around 10,000ft, the air is too thin to breathe and stay conscious for long. Occasionally, however, things can go wrong. The cabin pressurisation may fail, or there may be an explosive decompression, when the cabin air is sucked out rapidly.

Either way, you will be in trouble above 10,000ft if you don't get some oxygen quickly. Oxygen masks are stored in either the overhead sections or, occasionally, in the seat-backs. They are released automatically if cabin pressure fails. The elastic band fits around the back of the head, the mask fits over the nose and mouth and you simply breathe normally.

An important thing to remember is that you should always fit your own mask before attempting to help a child or infirm passenger. This may sound a bit harsh, but the reasoning is logical. If you don't get your own mask on, you may pass out before you have the chance to help the other person. That way, both lives are at risk. Get yourself breathing normally and then, even if the other person has lost consciousness, you will be able to get their mask on and they will soon be OK.

Whilst you are doing all this, the aircraft will be diving rapidly. This may be a frightening experience, but try to remember that the pilot is simply trying to get below 10,000ft or so as quickly as possible, so that everyone can breathe normally without the masks.

One final safety tip. Oxygen burns, so for pity's sake remember to put out your cigarette before placing the mask over your face!

Passports (see also *Check-In, Visas*)

More people forget to take their passport than any other item. Don't be one of them — you won't get far without it.

If you haven't already got one that hasn't expired (check now — I'll wait), then please make sure that you apply in plenty of time. The 'silly season' for passport applications is just before the summer holiday period, in June and July. Around this time, it might take several weeks to process your application. It's quicker if you do it personally, rather than by post, but be prepared for long queues. Normal passports, valid for 10 years, come in two different thicknesses. The common ones have 23 pages for visas, entry and exit stamps, whilst the thicker versions have 89 and are better suited to the frequent flyer.

Children of 16 or over will need their own passport, but up to that age they can be included on that of a parent. Children do not need photographs, but everyone else does. The quickest, easiest and cheapest way is to use one of those do-it-yourself photographic booths at railway stations and other places. It won't look anything like you, but don't worry. When you've travelled

Pitch

halfway round the world to present it to a strange immigration officer, you won't look anything like you either! The best way of doing it is to walk all night through the wind and rain, then go and have your photo taken at dawn. The immigration officer will recognise you immediately!

When you are in a foreign country, treat your passport like gold. Don't let it out of your sight. They are common quarry for thieves and the loss of one causes a great deal of hassle. You have been warned!

Pitch (see also *Roll, Stalls, Yaw*)

The pitch of the aircraft is its rotation about a line drawn through the length of its wings. If that sounds a bit complicated, the pitch tells you whether the nose is up (climbing) or down (diving). Better?

The pitch is controlled by the elevators and engine thrust. The two have to work together. If the joystick is pulled back too far when the engine thrust is

| Flying straight and level | Climbing - wings level | Climbing and turning left |
| Diving - wings level | Diving and turning right | Your passengers have just spilled their drinks ! |

THE ARTIFICIAL HORIZON

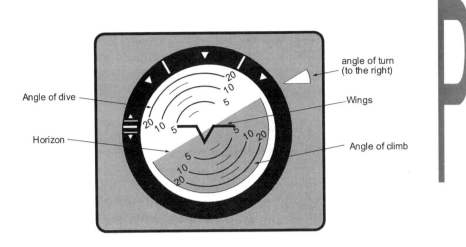

THE ARTIFICIAL HORIZON DURING A LEVEL TURN TO THE RIGHT

low, the nose will rise without sufficient power to maintain airspeed. Under these conditions, an aircraft might reach its stalling speed. Modern fly-by-wire aircraft such as the Airbus series have on-board computers that continuously monitor the performance of the aircraft to prevent this from happening. If the stick is pulled back too far in one of these planes, the computer automatically compensates by increasing engine thrust to keep the plane airborne.

The main instrument used by a pilot for monitoring pitch is the Artificial Horizon. This contains a small representation of the aircraft seen from the rear, together with a line marking the horizon, which can move. If the little plane is above the line, the aircraft is nose-up. If it is below it, it is nose-down. Since the horizon line can tilt, this instrument will also show the degree of bank or roll.

Primary Flight Controls (see also *Fly-By-Wire, Pitch, Roll, Yaw, Yoke*)

Otherwise known as the elevator, aileron and rudder, these devices control the plane's flight.

The elevator is the hinged portion on the trailing edge of the horizontal tail section. It is controlled by pushing forwards or pulling backwards on the joystick and causes the aircraft to respectively dive or climb.

The ailerons are similar hinged parts on the trailing edge of the wings. They make the aircraft roll into a bank, thereby allowing it to turn to change direction. The ailerons are controlled by moving the joystick from side to side, moving it left to bank to the left and right to bank to the right.

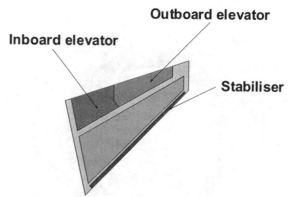

Inboard elevator

Outboard elevator

Stabiliser

The elevators of a 747.

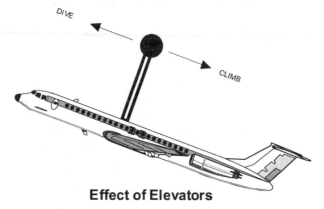

DIVE

CLIMB

Effect of Elevators

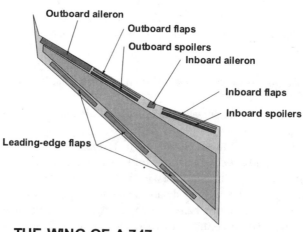

Outboard aileron

Outboard flaps

Outboard spoilers

Inboard aileron

Inboard flaps

Inboard spoilers

Leading-edge flaps

THE WING OF A 747

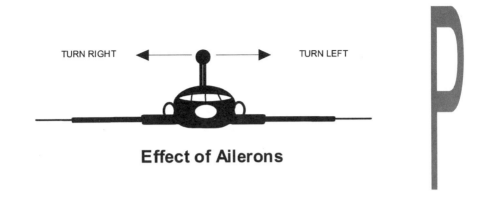

Effect of Ailerons

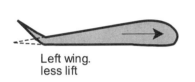

Left wing.
less lift

E AILERONS IN A BANK TO THE LEFT

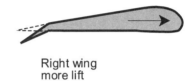

Right wing
more lift

THE AILERONS IN A BANK TO THE LEFT

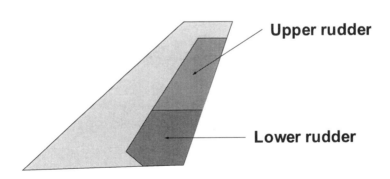

Upper rudder

Lower rudder

The tail of a 747.

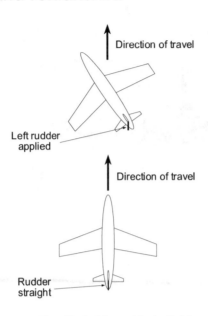

Direction of travel

Left rudder
applied

Direction of travel

Rudder
straight

The effect of the rudder in flight

Many people think that the rudder is used for turning, as on a boat. This is not so. Applying rudder in flight (done by the pilot's feet on two pedals) causes the aircraft to 'yaw'. This means that it still moves in the same direction, but is turned as it moves. A bit like a car skidding on ice. The rudder does turn the plane, however, when it is taxying on the ground. Different designs of aircraft need different amounts of rudder to be applied in a turn to prevent sideslipping.

You are now a fully-qualified pilot. Next week — how to build your own fast breeder nuclear reactor!

Push-Back

A modern jetliner, sleek, elegant and powerful though it is, usually has a rather cumbersome start to its travels. When everyone is aboard, the doors have been closed and the jetway rolled back, a strange-looking vehicle, low with extraordinarily large wheels, is connected to the nosewheel struts by a push bar. The vehicle then pushes the aircraft backwards to the main part of the apron, where it will taxi to the runway under its own power. That's all there is to a push-back.

The alternative to a push-back is a power-back. In some cases an airliner will use the reverse-thrust capability of its engines to move itself from the jetway to the apron. It then switches to conventional forward thrust to taxi to the runway.

Queues (see also *Check-In, Immigration*)

They say that the British love to queue. I'm British. I don't! Unfortunately, when it comes to air travel, queues are unavoidable. Let's have a look at the number of times you are likely to have to queue during a typical trip.

We'll start off by being generous and assuming that you are already in the

How can something so small push something so big?

terminal and haven't had to queue so far. Now you need to check-in. Queue number 1. Next, it's time to go through to the departure lounge. Queue number 2 is to show your boarding card. Queue number 3 is for the security check. Number 4 is at passport control. Now you've made it to the departure lounge. When it's time to board the aircraft, there's queue number 5. At the end of your flight, queue number 6 is to get off the aircraft. Number 7 is usually the longest of all and is for immigration into the country you are visiting. Queue number 8 is for customs and then you are out. How many times you queue after that depends on whether you have a chauffeur-driven limo or need to take three buses, two trains and a ferry!

I have made many short flights where the time that I spent in queues has been longer than the time that I spent in the air. I suppose it's all part of life's rich pageant!

Radar (see also *Air Traffic Control, Navigation, Weather*)

The principle of radar (radio detection and ranging) is very simple. A radio signal is sent out from a transmitter. If it encounters a solid or reasonably solid object, the radio waves are reflected back and picked up by a receiver. The results are usually displayed on a screen, which shows the position of aircraft, clouds, birds or anything else that reflects the signal.

There are several different types of radar. Long-range radar is used by air traffic control to monitor planes in the air. During a transatlantic trip, something like 10 stations will have followed the aircraft for most of its journey. Ground radar at airports monitors the complex pattern of aircraft movements on the apron, taxiways and runways. Radar on board the aircraft itself, mounted inside the nose-cone, is used for both ground-mapping and storm cloud detection. In a 747, the range is switchable from 30-300 miles and the beam can be directed from the flightdeck. The crew can spot landfall from a

R

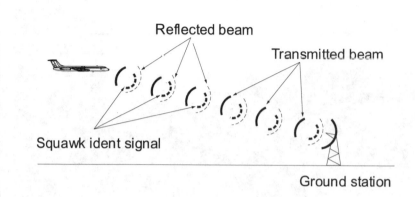

The Principle of RADAR

distance of around 100 miles and another aircraft from around 20. If storms are seen ahead on the flight path, the pilot will request permission to change course and fly around them.

Radio (see also *Air Traffic Control*)

The flight deck is in VHF radio contact with a controller for virtually the whole of the flight. From clearance to start engines, to shutdown on arrival, the Captain will have talked to and exchanged information with a variety of control centres. During the flight itself, he will have reported his position and height every hour. The aircraft will have received updated weather reports every 30min.

A radio transponder in the plane can also be switched on to respond to

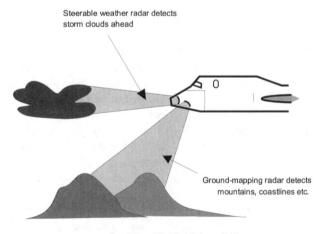

On-board RADAR in a 747

incoming radar waves from the ground and transmit a signal, identifying the aircraft's flight number and altitude. Back in the control centre, this information appears on the radar screen alongside the 'blip' from the aircraft itself. This is called the 'squawk ident'.

Radio is also used for navigation. The pilot has VHF distance measuring equipment and ground radio beacons which enable him to locate his precise position.

The total number of aerials on a 747 is quite formidable. In addition to three VHF aerials, the two air traffic control antennae and three distance measuring aerials, it will have two automatic direction finders, a marker beacon antenna, two high frequency and two omni-directional aerials. Also fitted are two satellite communications systems and finally two localiser and two glide slope antennae for the automatic landing systems.

Reservations (see also *Bumping, Latest Check-In Time, Tickets*)

It is a common misconception that, provided you have a reservation for a flight, you are guaranteed a seat whatever happens.

First of all, it is vital that you show up before the latest check-in time, regardless of the actual departure time of the aircraft. Secondly, checking-in towards the end of the allowed time slot will usually mean that your choice of seat is restricted. A party may not be able to sit together or a smoker may be forced to take a non-smoking seat. The latter is a common occurrence these days, since airlines have dramatically

reduced the number of smoking seats available, and they are normally allocated quickly.

Finally, all airlines overbook. Yes, they actually sell more tickets than there are seats on the plane. If that sounds a bit dim, it is necessary because of the large number of people, especially business users, who do not turn up for the flight. These are known as 'no-shows'. If the airlines only sold as many tickets as there are seats, the 'no-shows' would mean that the plane might be half-empty. Clearly, the financial consequences for the airline could be disastrous.

So if you really want to fly, show up in plenty of time.

Roll (see also *Dutch Roll, Pitch, Yaw*)

This could be what you have for lunch on a short flight, but I was thinking more in terms of the movement of an aircraft when one wing is raised and the other lowered. It is the way an aircraft turns and, as such, is a bit on the important side. The degree of roll is controlled by the ailerons and operated by moving the control column from side to side.

I love to watch passengers who haven't flown much before, when they are sitting in a window seat on the side whose wing is going down. Pilots normally try to make very shallow turns so as not to worry those of a nervous disposition. There are times, though, particularly when turning for the final approach into some airports, where space is restricted and the turn has to be tight. The look of terror as they find themselves staring at the ground is followed as a rule by a lean in the seat so that they are almost upright, but sideways to the plane! A whole batch of them sitting together is a really comical sight! There's no need to bother anyway. The forces on the aircraft mean that you are still being pressed squarely into your seat, even when the wings are almost vertical. Leaning over won't change anything but it will make you uncomfortable.

Roll

Runway (see also *Airports, Take-Off, Major UK Airports*)

This is a long piece of tarmac or concrete that planes take off and land on. Next subject.

What do you mean — you already knew that? You want more details or you'll put this wretched book back on the shelf? You shouldn't be this far into it if you're not going to buy it.

Oh, all right then. More details. You've asked for it.

You may have noticed that all runways have numbers painted on their surface at both ends. This indicates their direction on a magnetic compass. So Runway 9 will run due east (90°), Runway 27 will run due west (270°) etc. Since runways are straight, it doesn't take a superbrain to work out that if one end of a runway has a 9 on it, then the other end will have a 27 on it!

Runways are lit at night, but also have a series of coloured lights on the approach end, cleverly designed to let the pilot know if he is coming in at the correct height at any time. This is known as the glide slope.

Most international airports have several runways. This allows simultaneous take-offs and landings and also lets aircraft take off and land in the best direction for the prevailing wind. Some airports, however, including some very busy ones, somehow get by with just one. The supreme example of this has to be London Gatwick. It is quite usual for an aircraft waiting to take off there to have to queue just off the end of the runway, until another one coming in has landed.

The length of an airport's runways govern which types of aircraft can use it. A fully-laden Boeing 747 needs a much longer take-off run than a smaller plane. A Jumbo, in fact, seems to take for ever to get airborne. One of the common fears of inexperienced passengers is that the aircraft is simply going to run out of runway. In fact, the take-off run lasts for only around 45-55sec, depending on the weight of the aircraft. The weight is made up of people, luggage and fuel. A full flight, therefore, going all the way non-stop to Hong Kong will definitely be at the heavy end of the allowable weight range. Don't worry about it, though. Runways have to be long enough not only for take-off but also for aborted take-offs up to the speed known as V1.

The most frightening runways are those built out into the sea. When taking off, the water looks awfully close as you run out of runway. When landing, it's worse. The plane is getting lower and lower and you can't see the runway as a passenger because you can't, of course, look forwards. Just when you think that the wheels are getting wet, terra firma appears below and you heave a sigh of relief. The only airline I know of that once did something about this was American Airlines. They installed a video camera in the cockpit, looking forwards so that everyone had a pilot's eye view. Tremendous idea. I haven't seen one recently, so maybe they have stopped doing it. If so, I can't think why.

Runways in the Third World can be in a terrible state at times. Many aren't even flat, and potholes are not uncommon. Aircraft do, however, have very heavy-duty suspension systems and so the odd hump or depression is neither dangerous nor uncomfortable.

Scheduled Flights (see also *Chartered Aircraft, Tickets*)

Lots of passengers who fly only to holiday destinations never realise that there are flights that operate to a regular timetable. These are known as scheduled flights and have to fly unless there is a very good reason for not doing. That's why they are far more expensive than chartered flights, which can do all sorts of deals to maximise the number of passengers.

I remember flying back from the States with Pan Am several times just after the Lockerbie disaster. The economy cabin was almost deserted every time. Great news for me, since I was able to take a centre seat block, raise all the arm-rests and use it as a bed! Not so good news for the airline, though, which had to fly almost empty. The losses must have been terrific.

Seats (see also *Check-In*)

One of the decisions you will have to make at check-in is whether you want a window or aisle seat. If, for some reason (such as the M25) you are late checking-in for your flight, you will probably be lumbered with a centre seat if you are flying a wide-bodied jet. Smaller aircraft often have only two seats beside each other and so this problem cannot arise. Seating patterns vary from airline to airline and class to class, so it is always advisable to ask for details at the check-in desk.

Where you decide to sit is always a matter of personal preference, but the choice of seat type can be

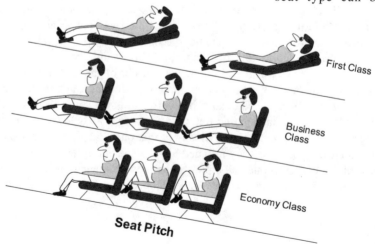

First Class

Business Class

Economy Class

Seat Pitch

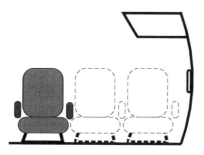

The Aisle Seat.

Choose this if you have a weak bladder
or like to go walkabout in-flight.

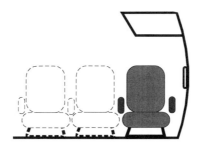

The Window Seat.

Choose this if you are a sleeper
or just want to be left alone.

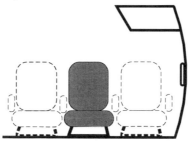

The Centre Seat.

Choose this if you:
a) like to annoy other people
b) like other people to annoy you
c) have no arms

S

important. Those people, for instance, cursed with weak bladders should avoid window seats on long-haul flights! Nature always calls at the worst possible time and this is usually when the person sitting next to you in the aisle seat has just been given his tray and hors d'oeuvres for the evening meal. Meals always last for an age in aircraft and it is totally impossible to weave your way past a dining passenger without covering him in food! If, however, (like me) you are the sort who likes to get some sleep on a flight and does not like being disturbed, choose a window seat. If you find yourself sitting next to the aisle and trying desperately to get some sleep, you can bet that the person sitting next to you is the one with the weak bladder! It's also worth remembering that the snoozers amongst us will have a slightly easier time in a window seat because you can rest your head against the side of the fuselage. Always put a pillow between you and it, though — you will be amazed how much it vibrates! Of course, if you are an aircraft 'yuppie' you will already have one of those specially-shaped inflatable neck pillows that let you sleep anywhere and at any angle (if you believe what's written on the box). I must confess that I have got one, but have never plucked up the courage to use it. It's not the pillow itself — it's having to blow it up in a crowded aircraft that I just can't bring myself to do. Psychiatrists would have a field day with me!

Centre seats — the ones with at least a window seat one side and an aisle seat on the other — are to be avoided like the plague! There's a constant battle to decide whose arm rest is whose, you can't sleep, you are always having to get up to let someone out and you often find that cabin attendants ignore you. The problem is that centre seats are often in the middle of the aircraft and cabin attendants take one side each. Each one, therefore, leaves you to the other. Take my word for it. Centre seats are the pits!

Seat Belts (see also *Emergency Landings*)

Aircraft seat belts were designed by a committee. They must have been. Your first sight of them will be as you are shown to your seat. The 'fasten seat belts' sign is on and so, like the good little passenger that you are, you try to fasten yours, even though people are still coming on board and the engines aren't even running yet.

You won't be able to fasten it, because the two ends that you have will not fit into each other, no matter how much brute force you apply. A quick examination of the problem reveals that both ends are the same. You glance over to the guy sitting in the next seat. He's trying to fit two identical ends together as well. A quick swap and they click together good as gold. The only problem now is that yours is twisted. That means that the buckle will dig into your stomach the minute that you pull it tight. When you untwist it, it won't click together anymore. The only way that you can make it fit is by twisting the other side of it. Back to square one.

When you go to pull it tight, you realise that with the size it is now it would fit across the midriff of a bull elephant! Where do all the incredibly fat people go that must have used the seat before you? You saw everyone get off the plane when it arrived. Every one looked more or less normal. And how on earth did they ever fit into the seat in the first place? Just as you are pondering these deep philosophical questions, a very fat man gets on board. His seat belt wouldn't fit round a beanpole! It's at that minute that you realise what happens. The girls at the check-in desk, the ones that give you your seat assignment, have a good look at you and measure you up. If you look like Olive Oyl, they give you a seat that a Sumo wrestler just got out of. And vice versa. Clever, aren't they?

What are the seat belts for? Well, they certainly do a good job of keeping you in your seat when the ride gets a bit choppy. Since clear-air turbulence can happen at any time, it's always a good idea to keep your belt loosely fastened throughout the flight. The cabin attendants have enough to do without peeling you off the roof.

Apart from that, I've always had the feeling that a lap-type seat belt is really not good enough in an emergency. Recent research has shown that this type of belt does nothing to prevent serious injury to the head, both by contact with the seat in front and by whiplash. One school of thought is that the seats should be rear-facing, as they are in military personnel carriers, but others consider that the damage caused by hand-baggage flying forwards into passengers' faces would be a problem. The dangers would certainly be reduced if 'full-harness' belts, with both lap and shoulder restraints were fitted in all aircraft. After all, if it's good enough for the pilot...

Security (see also *Bombs*)

Airports and airlines have, in recent years, become very security-conscious. Hijackings, bombings and airport massacres have cost hundreds of lives. Sometimes, to the bona fide fare-paying passenger, the security measures now taken seem a little bit over-the-top. But it has to be worth any amount of inconvenience to reduce, and hopefully eliminate, the risks of terrorist activity.

So what are you likely to encounter on the way to your seat? If you are flying overseas, you will need to show your passport at check-in. That will prove that you are the person shown on the ticket. You will also be asked some questions about your luggage. Some of the questions may sound a bit odd, but please take them seriously. The check-in staff will. Then, as you wait to go through to the departure lounge, you are bound to see armed security guards and/or policemen. Leave any of your suitcases unattended briefly and they are likely to attract the attention of these people. You could have some explaining to do.

Security at Birmingham Airport — if the alarm beeps, you will be searched manually.

Passing through to the departure lounge, you will need to show your boarding card and passport, and you will have to walk through a gate which detects metal objects electronically. If the beeper beeps, you will have to be searched either manually or with a hand-held detector. To save time and inconvenience, therefore, it's a good idea to hand over anything that might set off the alarm before you walk through. A tray is usually provided for the purpose. The most common items that set off the alarms are bunches of keys and loose change, but don't forget spectacle cases, pocket watches, metal combs, pens and pencils. I used to have a leather jacket with a rather chunky metal zip. It never failed to get me caught!

Meanwhile, your baggage will have been X-rayed for suspicious items. If you are carrying anything that is X-ray opaque, or looks suspicious, you will be taken aside and asked to open the offending case or bag. You will usually be asked to switch on any electronic items such as calculators, computers, tape recorders, etc. to show that they work properly and are not designed for any sinister applications.

Your carry-on baggage will also have been X-rayed and, if cleared, will be loaded on to the aircraft.

When called for boarding, you will need to show your boarding card again. The attendants will perform a head count to ensure that everyone is on board, and the ground crew will make sure that everyone who has checked-in for the flight is accounted for. If it is found that a passenger has checked-in some items of luggage, but is not on board, attempts will be made to locate them. If they cannot be found, there will be a delay as their luggage is found and off-loaded.

Security measures are not designed to hinder. They are designed to safe-

guard lives. The government has
issued security advice for anyone travelling by air. It
is as follows:

Always pack your own bags and don't borrow seemingly empty bags from anyone else. Never leave any of your baggage unattended. Never check-in bags for other people. Never carry anything on to an aircraft for someone else. Put your name and destination address on the outside of your luggage. Home address details should be inside. Keep money, passport, traveller's cheques and other valuables with you in your hand-baggage. Don't carry large amounts of cash.

Sleeping (see also *In-Flight Entertainment, Night Flights*)

If you have been reading this book from the beginning, rather than dipping-in here and there to find the best bits, you will know by now that I am an expert sleeper. Turbulence, engine failure, lightning and the duty-free trolley — I can sleep through them all. I've always thought that the best cure for something I'd rather not be doing is to sleep through it. As a matter of fact, I'm asleep right now. That's why I would never settle for a local anaesthetic if a general one was on offer. I don't care how trivial the operation is, I just don't want to know about it. The same goes for flying. Although it isn't exactly unpleasant, a long-haul flight is, without doubt, extremely boring. So I sleep through as much of it as I possibly can. You can too, provided you follow these words of wisdom:

1) Make sure that you get a window seat. 2) Pester the cabin attendant for as many extra pillows and blankets as you need. 3) Extract the 'do not disturb' sticker from your amenity bag and turn it to show whether or not you want to be woken up for meals. 4) If you are of North American descent, also extract the eye shades. No one else need bother. 5) Pad the side of the seat and fuse-lage with plenty of pillows to damp down the vibration and keep your head

upright. Fail to do this and you will wake up with a neck that thinks it's been hanged! 6) Stop worrying about anything. There's nothing you can do, so go to sleep.

Incidentally, there's a rumour currently circulating that airlines actually want us poor passengers to sleep, to give the cabin attendants a break. So the Captain, it appears, deliberately turns up the cabin temperature by around 5° as soon as the meal is finished, usually as the film is about to start. It's been called the 'Air Cosh'. If it's true, this form of mass sedation must be quite effective. I know that I certainly have difficulty staying awake during that part of a flight, and a quick glance around the cabin usually reveals that my fellow passengers are similarly afflicted. The airlines, of course deny that the temperature increases are to save the feet of the cabin crew, insisting that they are only to prevent passengers from waking up cold. We'll probably never know!

Smoke Hoods (see also *Emergency Evacuations*)

There has been much talk in recent years of the pros and cons of fitting smoke hoods in aircraft. In particular, the Manchester Airport disaster brought the whole subject into the public eye.

Certainly, there are many inflammable materials used in the interior of aircraft. Most of these, it would seem, tend to give off vast quantities of dense acrid smoke as they burn. People have undoubtedly been killed as a result of smoke inhalation. It seems to be a matter of common sense, therefore, to provide smoke hoods for all passengers. The authorities were saying a little while ago that there are many different types of hood, some being better than others. Until the best type was found, they would not be provided on the ground that they may inspire over-confidence. Now I don't know about you, but my thoughts on this are twofold. Firstly, any smoke hood must be better than none, and secondly, if I found myself in the middle of a burning fuselage, over-confidence is not the first emotion that would come to mind!

OK, so I have to pay a couple of quid extra for my ticket. Give me non-inflammable seats and smoke hoods now!

"When they asked if I wanted a smoke hood, I wasn't expecting this!

Sound Barrier (see also *Concorde*)

Not really a barrier at all, of course. We know that now, thanks to the pioneering efforts of the US military pilot Chuck Yeager, who flew his X-1 rocket plane to Mach 1.07 on 14 October 1947. On that date, the first sonic boom was heard on Earth.

The Mach number is the airspeed of the aircraft divided by the speed of sound at that altitude. The speed of sound is always therefore Mach 1.0. If, for instance, the speed of sound is 700 mph and your airspeed is 560 mph, then the Mach number is 560/700, or 0.8. Similarly, if the airspeed is 840 mph, your Mach number is 840/700 or 1.2 and you are flying supersonically.

Before Yeager's time, there were fears that the speed of sound was a real barrier, and that an aircraft might break up as it flew at Mach 1. Certainly, Yeager's earlier flights in the X-1, which was dropped from the belly of a B-29 bomber at around 20,000ft, tended to show that the nearer the aircraft came to approaching the speed of sound, the more violently it was shaken around. As things transpired, the ride became beautifully smooth at Mach 1 and the whole thing was something of an anti-climax.

The compression of air in front of the aircraft as it approaches Mach 1 causes turbulence and eventually the shock wave that is the sonic boom. The problems experienced by Yeager have now been overcome by special wing and fuselage design, and the ride through the sound barrier is so smooth that you would never know it had happened if it weren't for the machmeter.

Mach 1, the speed of sound, is not a constant number. At sea-level, it is around 760 mph, but the speed of sound decreases with increasing altitude up to around 35,000ft. At the altitude that Yeager flew, Mach 1 is about 654 mph. Even the lumbering 747 cruises at around 550 mph, which is Mach 0.83 at 35,000ft.

Like the 4-minute mile, breaking the sound barrier was more of a psycho-logical problem than a physical one. These days, both of these records are broken regularly. Virtually all military hardware, and Concorde, are designed specifically to fly supersonic and the whole thing has become routine. The difficulty was in being the first to do it, without knowing what lay ahead.

Stalls (see also *Airspeed*)

Your aircraft has a stalling speed. Well, several, actually, depending on the wing configuration and other factors. The important thing, however, is that it cannot fly below its stalling speed. The reason is that the airflow over the wings, which generates lift, is simply not sufficient to hold the aircraft up below the stall speed.

If you think that this sounds a bit on the dangerous side, you're absolutely right. At least, near the ground it is. If you stall at a great enough altitude, you

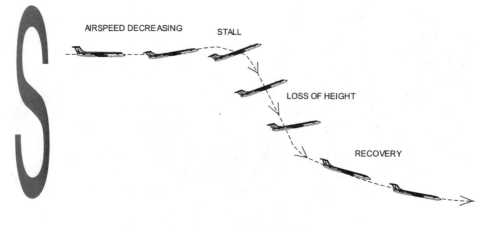

AIRSPEED DECREASING   STALL

LOSS OF HEIGHT

RECOVERY

THE STALL

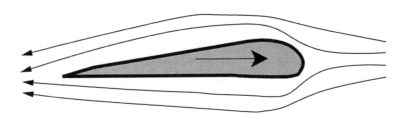

Airflow over the wing in normal flight

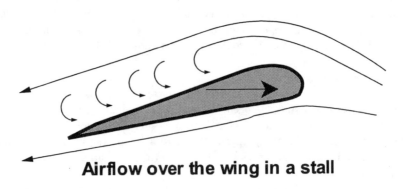

Airflow over the wing in a stall

will simply lose some height as the aircraft falls, the nose will drop, the speed will increase and the wings will unstall. The problem comes, of course, if you hit the ground before the wings have unstalled!

Stalling speed is highest when the wings are flying 'clean', with all flaps retracted, during the climb and cruise. To enable an aircraft to land slowly without stalling, flaps are used during the final descent. This also increases the drag on the wings, so you also get some buffeting. Fuel efficiency is also dramatically reduced.

Flaps will also be used on take-off, and gradually retracted bit-by-bit, as the aircraft gains speed. The trick is to make sure that the aircraft is travelling fast enough, since every time the flaps are retracted slightly, the stall speed is increased.

The crew on the flightdeck are very aware of the stalling speed of their aircraft under different conditions. They also have an audible stall warning and 'stick-shakers' that leave them in no doubt when they are close to reaching the stall speed. On the new 'fly-by-wire' aircraft, it is said to be impossible to stall, since the on-board computers take over if this is likely to happen. They then make the necessary adjustments to the controls to prevent the stall from happening. The pilots of the Airbus series aircraft are particularly proud of their airshow party trick, when they make a very low pass over the runway, very slowly and with the nose raised high in the air. This sort of manoeuvre would be the kiss of death to conventional aircraft, which would be operating below their stall conditions. The Airbus computers, however, keep the giant in the air in a very impressive demonstration.

Standby (see also *Tickets*)

The poor devil on standby has all the hassle of getting to the airport without knowing for certain whether he is going anywhere or not. The aircraft is officially full and he has to wait until after the latest check-in time to find out whether there are any no-shows.

On a long-haul route, it would be very unusual if there weren't any. Provided, therefore, that he is not too far down the list, the standby passenger has a pretty good chance of flying. Luckily, you can always count on some fool leaving it until the last minute and trying to get round the M25!

Take-Off (see also *Altitude*)

The take-off and initial climb can be quite disturbing to a passenger who is unused to it. The engines will be roaring until noise-abatement procedures, if any, are followed. There will be clunks as the undercarriage is retracted. Adjustments will be made to the flaps and turbulent air near the ground will cause buffeting of the aircraft. All this is perfectly normal. Nerves are always considerably eased if you know what to expect in advance, so let's go through the normal take-off and initial ascent sequence, commencing with the aircraft rolling down the runway.

The first critical speed is known as V1 and at this speed the Pilot is committed to take-off. The co-pilot calls out 'V1' and the aircraft continues to accelerate.

As the plane reaches VR, the speed at which it can become airborne, the pilot eases back on the control column in a process known as 'rotation'. The elevators lift and the nose of the aircraft rises, causing it gently to take to the air. If the rotation operation is performed too early, there is a serious danger of putting the aircraft into a stalling attitude, from which it will crash to the ground. The airspeed of the plane is therefore monitored closely during the take-off run, with the co-pilot calling out the critical speeds as they are reached.

There is an immediate sense of being airborne. Whilst not unpleasant, the 'floating' sensation of being in the air is very apparent. A 747, at this stage, will be climbing at an angle of about 9°, with an airspeed of around 180-190kts.

Shortly after VR, the speed known as V2 will be reached. It is now safe to climb, even with an engine failure. The most likely cause of engine problem these days on take-off is through a bird-strike. At Heathrow, for instance, there is, on average, one strike a week. Not all of them cause problems, of course, but birds are enough of a worry for all major airports to have special bird-scaring teams armed with the latest technical wizardry to ward off our feathered friends.

As soon as there is no usable runway left below the aircraft, the undercarriage will be retracted to reduce drag and increase the rate of climb. This is quite a noisy operation. There will be a whine of the hydraulic system,

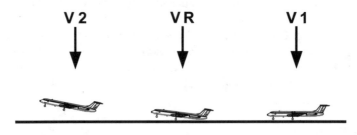

V 2

V R

V 1

At V 2, sufficient speed has built up to withstand an engine failure

At V R, the control column is pulled back to lift the nose

At V 1, the pilot is commited to take-off

THE TAKE - OFF

followed by two thumps as first the nosewheels and then the main wheels lock into the fuselage.

Just when you expect the engines to remain on full power, and while the ground still seems uncomfortably close, the pilot will almost certainly throttle back to observe local noise abatement procedures. The engines will sound as if they are losing power. Virtually all major airports have areas surrounding them where aircraft noise is regulated and closely monitored, for the benefit of local inhabitants.

Almost at the same time as engine power is reduced, the flaps will be partially retracted to further reduce drag. As this happens, there will probably be some 'sink' because the lift generated by the wings will also be lower. The change in engine tone and the sink feeling both contribute to the uninitiated passenger thinking that he is falling out of the sky!

After the flaps have been fully retracted, the plane is flying 'clean', and drag is reduced to a minimum. The airspeed will now normally increase to around 260-270kts. The autopilot will control the climb to the final flight level or to an intermediate level as instructed by air traffic control. The climb to cruising altitude will take about 40min.

In modern jets, the 'no-smoking' sign will be switched off only a few minutes after take-off but the 'fasten seat belt' sign will remain on for the initial climb, until the aircraft has flown through the lower cloud levels and into less turbulent air.

Tickets (see also *Latest Check-In Time, Reservations*)

If you book your flight as part of a package, or with plenty of time to spare, you will have your tickets with you as you arrive at the airport. Before you set off, however, please make sure that the date of travel, flight number, class of travel, destination and name of traveller are all correct. If they are, (and don't forget to check the return journey if you've booked one), then simply present the tickets to the check-in counter.

One of the most important bits of information on your ticket is the 'status'. It should say 'OK'. This means that you are a confirmed passenger. If it says 'WL' then you are a standby passenger.

Do not forget to reconfirm your onward or return ticket if you stay in one place for more than three days. In western countries, this can be done by telephone. In the more under-developed countries, however, where computers are either non-existent or just don't work, always do it in person and have your ticket officially stamped.

On the subject of tickets, how much did you pay for your flight? Ask that question to a full Jumbo and you will probably get as many different answers as there are passengers. It's an absolute jungle. A scheduled round trip to New York from London, for instance, can set you back anything between around

"I don't care if the small print **does** say it's the cabriolet version - I still want a roof on my plane!"

£300-£5,000. To do it as cheaply as possible, you will have to book something like 21 days in advance, travel mid-week and lose the right to a refund if you can't make the flights. If you've got the odd £5,000 to spare, you can turn up at the Concorde check-in desk 30min before the flight and return whenever you feel like it, since your ticket is valid for any Concorde you feel like flying back.

In between the two, there are a whole variety of fares. Apart from class of travel, there are Late-Savers, Super Apex, Promotion Apex and many others. Travel agents and Consolidators can normally get you a further discount by buying from the airlines in bulk.

Children occupying their own seat normally travel at 50% of the adult fare, although this can rise to as much as 75% in economy class with some airlines. Infants, who do not have their own seat, usually cost 10% of the adult price.

Time Differences (see also *International Date Line, Jet-Lag*)

For those who were too busy at school smoking behind the bike sheds or showering sixpences on 'Samantha no knickers', there now follows a brief geography lesson. It has to be brief — I was always at the front of Sam's queue lighting up a Woodbine!

It can't be midday everywhere in the world at once. There aren't enough suns to go round. When the sun is high over Great Britain, they are bashing out the Zs in Australia. The sun tracks from east to west over the skies, so time has to change from east to west so that the sun is always high in the sky at midday. So that we don't have to change our watches every time we move, some bright spark invented 'time-zones', which are chunks of the earth with the same time. The borders of the zones run more or less north-south, with some slight meanders for the sake of convenience.

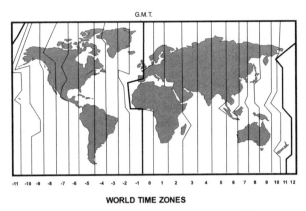

WORLD TIME ZONES

If your course is due north or south, therefore, you will not cross any time zones and there will be no time differences. If, on the other hand, you are flying east or west, you will cross over several zones, on each occasion changing the time by one hour. As you travel west, the time goes back. Travelling east, the time goes forward.

Jet-lag is always worst the more time-zones that are crossed in flight, because the time changes much faster than the body can compensate for.

That was really interesting wasn't it? Excuse me while I light up and find Sam's telephone number.

Turbulence (see also *Radar, Weather*)

Picture the scene. There I am, lounging back in my seat with a glass full of beer. The 747 is cruising along at 35,000ft and the sky is a brilliant clear blue. Down below, the ground can be seen in minute detail. Not a cloud in sight. The seat belt signs are off and everyone is thinking how easy this flying business is.

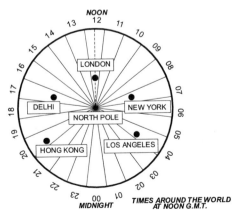

TIMES AROUND THE WORLD AT NOON G.M.T.

Ork

The Effect of heavy turbulence!

Suddenly, the aircraft loses 10ft. It's like being in an express lift. Instantaneously, your stomach and beer are stuck to the ceiling. Passengers scream and hold on to their seat with a vice-like grip. Then, just as quickly, the plane bounces back the same 10ft as it hits an equally vicious up-draught of air. Back comes your stomach. Back comes your beer — all over you. Dear reader, you have just encountered clear-air turbulence.

It's not usually that bad, of course. Clear-air turbulence (CAT) usually just means a choppy ride for a few minutes. The problem with CAT, though, is that you never know where it is, and neither does the pilot. Normal turbulence goes hand-in-hand with storm clouds and weather fronts, and these the crew can pick up on their weather radar. Not so with CAT. Like the Spanish Inquisition, you never expect it and it can strike at any time. CAT is one good reason why it's sensible to take the advice of the crew and always wear your seat belt loosely fastened, even when the seat belt sign is switched off. Better to have your beer and drink it too than your head hit the ceiling!

Undercarriage (see also *Landings*)

The undercarriage of a 747 is a very impressive piece of engineering. It has to be. Coming in to land, a 747 will still weigh around 200 tons, even when empty of fuel. All this is to be supported on 18 wheels!

The main undercarriage consists of 16 wheels on four separate struts, known as oleo legs. These legs provide the suspension necessary to cushion the impact forces, and also are calibrated to weigh the aircraft when taxying out for take-off. The two nosewheels are mounted on one strut.

SO, GENTLEMEN - THIS IS THE NEW UNDERCARRIAGE DESIGN FOR EMERGENCY LANDINGS ON ROOFTOPS.

When down, the undercarriage increases the drag of the aircraft. It is, therefore, retractable and is raised into the fuselage nacelles shortly after take-off. The two hefty thumps as the main undercarriage retracts and the smaller ones as the nosewheels come up can be frightening to the uninitiated, but are really nothing to worry about. Undercarriage up is signalled in the cockpit by three red lights.

The nosewheel is steerable for low-speed manoeuvring on the ground. The brakes can be controlled either automatically or manually by the pilot, using the tips of the rudder pedals.

Vapour Trails (see also *Altitude, Weather*)

Most of us spot jets from the ground by the appearance of vapour trails in the sky. If you live close to Heathrow or Gatwick, you will know that they are there when your windows shatter!

Vapour trails are actually water droplets or small ice crystals. As the engine burns jet fuel, it produces, amongst other things, water vapour as a gas. This hot water vapour is shot out of the exhaust, where it cools and condenses to form liquid water droplets or ice, depending on the outside temperature. That becomes the vapour trail, which is, in effect, a thin but very long cloud.

The life of a vapour trail can vary enormously. On some days, when the upper atmosphere is still, they can be very persistent. It is not unusual to see the trails criss-crossing, as successive aircraft leave their feathery footprints across the heavens. Now wasn't that poetic? Ah, well — back to reality!

Water condensing out of the engine exhaust produces those beautiful vapour trails we are so used to seeing.

Visas (see also *Passports*)

Always check whether any of the countries you are intending to visit requires an entrance visa. If so, you won't get in without it. The other piece of advice I have is don't leave it until the last minute to apply for one. Some, particularly those from the more exotic countries, take a long time to come through. Even worse, some of the smaller countries are not represented in the UK. In these cases, applications need to be made through other nearby countries where diplomatic representatives are stationed; Paris or Rome for example. If you think that there might be hassle in obtaining the visa you require, then it might be a good idea to go through one of the independent visa agencies. They will charge for their services, but they will also do all the work.

When in the country concerned, always observe the visa conditions. In particular, if you need to visit a country more than once, make sure that your visa is valid for multiple entries. Many visas allow only one entrance and exit.

Don't outstay your welcome and make sure that you have been properly logged out of the country when you leave. I was once refused entrance to the US because their records showed that I hadn't left after my previous trip. I was a wanted man!

Finally, some countries require an exit visa, especially for longer stays. Make sure that you check, before stepping on to foreign soil.

Weather (see also *Delays, Radar*)

The biggest influence on your journey is likely to be the weather. It can disrupt departure times, cause routeing changes and can even close your destination airport, forcing the pilot to make a landing at a safe alternative.

Take-off is a relatively straightforward process, the main problem being with fog. Fog is, of course, usually just a cloud on the ground, often mixed with smoke, dust and other pollutants to form smog.

It is still a major problem at most British and European Airports. Not that it affects the actual landing anymore. Even in zero visibility, your plane could be brought in on a full Category 3 ILS instrument landing to a beautifully smooth touchdown. The problem is what follows the touchdown — taxying to the apron or jetway. For safety reasons, therefore, visibility limits of a cloud base greater than 50ft and visibility greater than 220yd are imposed. If your destination airport has a lower cloud base or shorter visibility, your plane will be directed to an alternative landing site. Coaches will usually then be laid on to complete your journey.

Although the take-off run can be made in principle with very limited visibility, the complexity of the ground movements at most major airports dictates that they be closed in thick fog. Delays in departing aircraft must always be expected on foggy days. It should also be remembered that many departing aircraft will only recently have arrived at the airport from somewhere else. Landing delays can, therefore, have a knock-on effect and cause departure delays.

Many airports have to be closed through the effects of snow. Although snow-melting equipment is available at all large airports likely to receive snow, there will inevitably be a delay before runways can be opened after a heavy snowfall. Slush under the wheels can seriously restrict the ability of an aircraft to accelerate and take off safely.

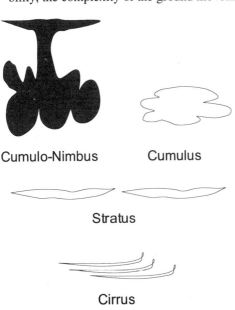

Cumulo-Nimbus   Cumulus

Stratus

Cirrus

Common Cloud Types

Landing poses similar problems in that incoming aircraft can skid over an icy, snowbound or slushy runway.

Low cloud is less of a problem than it used to be, with the new navigational equipment that allows full automatic landings. Even in this day and age, though, airports can still close if the cloud base is very low and the cloud cover thick.

Clouds seem to cause more passenger nervousness than almost anything else. Which is strange when you consider that they are not solid objects at all. They do look disconcertingly solid, though, as the aircraft gets nearer and nearer to the unbroken white mass as it begins its descent.

There are several different types of cloud and most of them are completely harmless, apart from causing mild turbulence. The type that form layers, with a more or less straight top and bottom, are called 'stratus'. Those that pile up into large heaps towering into the sky are known as 'cumulus'. The very high feathery clouds go by the name of 'cirrus'.

Sometimes, the prefixes 'alto' or 'cirro' are used to denote cloud height. 'Alto' means a low cloud between 6-20,000ft, whilst 'cirro' is used for higher clouds between 20-40,000ft. The word 'nimbo' or 'nimbus' means rain. So both cumulo-nimbus and nimbo-stratus are rain clouds.

Stratus clouds are relatively stable and can persist only in still air. Cumulus clouds mark rising and falling air and so give you a dose of the bumps. The general rule is the whiter and fluffier the cloud, the more gentle is the ride. As they get greyer and more solid, the need for seat belts increases.

The one to watch out for is the heavy storm cloud known as cumulo-nimbus. It's easy to spot. It rises like a massive tower from cumulus clouds and its top is flat and overhanging to form the shape of a giant anvil. These clouds have a hectic interior. Air currents hurl water droplets up and down, building up static electricity which is discharged as lightning. Water that is flung high enough into the cloud can become supercooled and will form ice on anything solid that touches it.

Hail, which is frozen water, can damage aircraft. Most hail is relatively small, but each time a frozen water droplets rises or falls through a cold enough cloud, another layer of water will freeze on to it, making the hail ball bigger. Hail that has been thrown up and down through a large cumulo-nimbus several times can be as big as a tennis ball!

The final type of cloud, and the one which has been responsible for more aircraft accidents than any other, is the cloud on the ground, or fog. In the days when all landings were manual, a bank of fog at the wrong time could completely disorient a pilot. Modern instrument landing systems, however, mean that a pilot can now safely land his aircraft when he can't see the nose!

Once in the air, the weather is less of a problem, since the jet flies above most of it. The pilot will, however, make course changes to avoid particularly heavy banks of cumulo-nimbus and their associated electrical storms. He will

also try to avoid strong head winds, which slow down groundspeed and burn up fuel. This he will often do by changing altitude, since many wind systems are confined to particular heights in the atmosphere. The only other disturbance he is likely to encounter is clear-air turbulence. There is very little he can do about this, although minor changes in course may be made if the ride is getting particularly choppy.

Winds can also be a problem when landing. Ideally, a landing should be made into a steady head wind, allowing an approach with a low groundspeed whilst still maintaining sufficient airspeed to remain aloft. Crosswinds, particularly when gusting, can be difficult. Sudden changes of wind direction, known as wind shear, can be very dangerous.

Wind Shear (see also *Weather*)

Wind shear has almost certainly been a problem since the early days of aviation, but has only recently been classed as a problem in its own right.

The effect of wind shear, in which the speed or direction, or both, of the wind suddenly changes, can be catastrophic at low altitudes. An aircraft coming in to land with a head wind can suddenly find that the direction shears round a full 180° to produce a tail wind. Under these circumstances, the airspeed of the plane drops dramatically and can fall below its stalling speed. This is precisely what happened to Delta flight 191, a Lockheed 1011 TriStar, at Dallas Fort Worth airport in August 1985.

Wind shear sensors are now fitted at all major airports and new control systems, both on-board and ground-based, are helping to detect the phenomenon quickly and accurately.

Wings (see also *Aircraft, Jet Engines, Primary Flight Controls*)

On my list of priorities, wings, I have to tell you, are right at the top. Just in front of engines. As long as the wings are intact and the engines are roaring, they can run out of Chicken Napoleon, Rum Babas and serve lukewarm lager. You won't hear me moan (well — not much anyway!). Even without engines, the wings can still bring you in to a perfectly respectable landing in an emergency. Since engines aren't much good without wings, the latter come top.

It is, of course, the wings that generate the lift required to get and keep you airborne. All they ask for is a steady flow of air over them and they will continue doing their job. That airflow is where the engines come in. Either during a climb, or in level flight, the engines move the aircraft forwards to create an airflow over the wings. During a descent, the nose is pitched down and the aircraft generates some or all of its own air-speed. This is how a glider works.

Lift is generated through a special shape of the wing in cross-section,

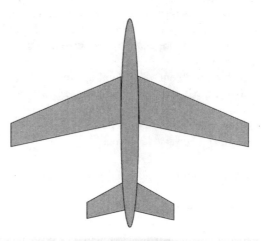

CONVENTIONAL
WING TYPE

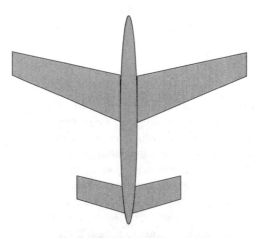

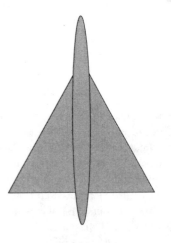

NEW SWEPT-FORWARD
WING TYPE

DELTA
WING TYPE

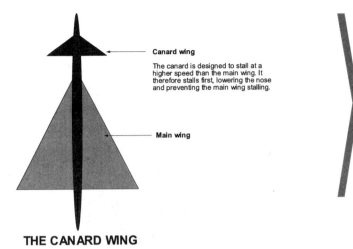

Canard wing

The canard is designed to stall at a higher speed than the main wing. It therefore stalls first, lowering the nose and preventing the main wing stalling.

Main wing

THE CANARD WING

known as an aerofoil. Air travelling over the wing is forced to travel further and faster than that going below it. Air pressure is therefore reduced above the wing, causing it to lift. The trick in wing design is to get the maximum amount of lift with the minimum amount of drag. It is possible, for instance, to greatly increase lift by extending the flaps. This, however, also greatly increases the drag. The effect of increased drag is a reduction in speed, greatly increased fuel consumption and a rather choppy ride.

Wing shape is important in determining flight characteristics. Having said that, the vast majority of airliners operating today have more or less the same design. The major exception is the delta wing of Concorde. Military aircraft show a much greater variety of wing type, including the variable-geometry type. These can be swept back close to the fuselage for high speed flight, or can be swung out for low speeds, take-offs and landings. Some have the small canard wings in front of the main wing to help stability.

The most efficient wing is said to be the swept-forward wing, but these are difficult to manufacture because of the enormous stresses placed on the wingtips. Some prototypes using this wing configuration have recently been made from the new lightweight composite materials that will feature strongly in the next generation of airliner.

X-Rays (see also *Security*)

Your baggage, both hand and checked-in, will be X-rayed before it is allowed on the aircraft. Modern western equipment is, these days, film-safe, so you shouldn't find your holiday photos ruined. Having said that, I always get as many films developed as possible before returning home. Besides eliminating any chance accidents, this has the bonus of forcing me to do it. Otherwise, I am quite likely to push the films in some drawer or other, only to remember

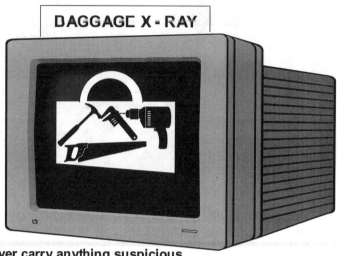

**Never carry anything suspicious
in your luggage !**

them several years later!

Be sensible in packing. Checked-in luggage should not contain any items that are likely to look suspicious when being X-rayed — transistor radios, cassette recorders, calculators, clocks and other electrical items fall into this category. If you must take this type of item with you, keep it in your hand-baggage and be prepared to show the examining officer that it works as it should.

Another thing that will arouse suspicion and may cause you to be delayed

Yaw

is any large X-ray opaque item that might be concealing something else. Do not carry any metal boxes.

Yaw (see also *Pitch, Primary Flight Controls, Roll*)

One of the three primary axes of movement of an aircraft — a plane is yawing when it is slewing sideways through the air without banking. Use of the rudder without the ailerons will cause yawing. It is often thought by the inexperienced that an aircraft can be turned using the rudder, in the same way that a boat can. Whilst this is true when the aircraft is taxying on the ground, it can only change direction in the air by banking with the ailerons (and supplementary use of the rudder). If the rudder alone is used, the nose of the aircraft will point in a different direction, but the aircraft itself will continue in the same direction. It is, if you like, skidding through the air.

Yoke (see also *Fly-By-Wire, Primary Flight Controls*)

Not the yellow of an egg. The yoke is another name for the control column that the pilot uses to manoeuvre the aircraft. It operates the elevators and ailerons. Pulled back towards the pilot, the elevators hinge up to raise the nose. Pushed forwards, the elevators lower and the nose drops. Turned to the left, the ailerons bank the plane to the left and turned right, it banks to the right. Shortly before take-off, the pilot will check for full and unobstructed movement of the yoke and control surfaces.

In older aircraft, the yoke is connected to the control surfaces by cables or hydraulic pipes. In the new technology 'fly-by-wire' machines, it is all done electronically. Currently under development is 'fly-by-light', in which the connections are made by fibre-optic links.

KEY

1 London Heathrow	6. Edinburgh
2 London Gatwick	7. Stansted
3 Birmingham	8. Manchester
4 East Midlands	9. Luton
5 Glasgow	10.Leeds/Bradford

The Major UK Airports

If you are flying from the UK, it's odds-on that you will be leaving from one of the airports described below. Businessmen who only fly long-haul intercontinental routes will usually only come to know and love Heathrow and Gatwick; our two biggest and busiest airports. Occasionally, they might find themselves flying from Manchester or Birmingham, the two provincial upstarts who are slowly but surely building up their long-haul traffic.

If, like me, you favour flying the Shuttle to the main departure airport, you will also know your local airport inside-out. It might be Manchester or Birmingham again, or it could be Glasgow, Edinburgh, East Midlands or Leeds/Bradford.

If, on the other hand, you are flying out to some exotic spot for a couple of weeks of packaged sun, charter flights may be leaving from somewhere you didn't even know had an airport! The charter flight favourites are still Gatwick and Luton, but Stansted, Birmingham, East Midlands, Manchester, Leeds/Bradford, Newcastle, Glasgow, Edinburgh and Bristol have their fair share. But what about Aberdeen, Blackpool, Bournemouth, Cardiff, Exeter, Kent, Liverpool, Norwich, Prestwick and Teesside?

Generally, the smaller the airport, the more I like it. A provincial terminal doesn't have the sheer excitement of Heathrow, but you don't need a bus to get round it. Smaller airports also have a much lower level of aircraft movements, so you tend to get the personal treatment a lot more. At the end of the day, you pays your money and you takes your choice.

Let's have a look at the major UK airports; how to get to them and what they've got to offer.

Birmingham International

Getting bigger all the time, Birmingham still has that friendly feel to it, but for how long? Superbly located and offering so many different destinations, Birmingham is a very useful airport. The original terminal is now used for cargo operations, since a new terminal was built on the other side of the airport in 1984. The 'new' terminal, now almost 10 years old, is currently being refurbished. The original control tower, though, is still in use. What looks like a new one at the new terminal is, in fact, apron control. The Eurohub Terminal was opened in 1991.

Getting there: dead easy. By road, it is signposted from both the M6 and M42. By train, frequent InterCity services take you to Birmingham International station, which is linked to the terminal by a Maglev monorail.

Facilities: both the main terminal and the new Eurohub contain restaurants, bars and shops.

Flights: frequent scheduled and charter flights by dozens of operators.

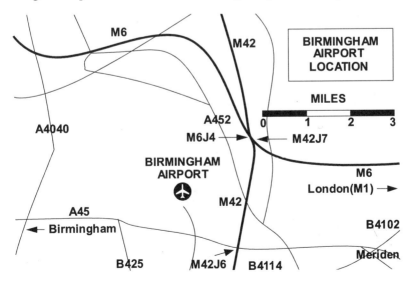

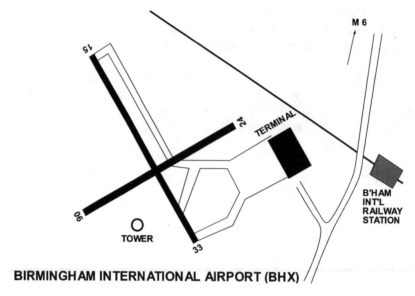

BIRMINGHAM INTERNATIONAL AIRPORT (BHX)

Bristol (Lulsgate)

Not really in the big league, but very useful if you live in the West Country and dislike long journeys to the airport.

Getting there: South of Bristol on the A38.

Facilities: Buffet and bar.

Flights: Both scheduled and charter flights.

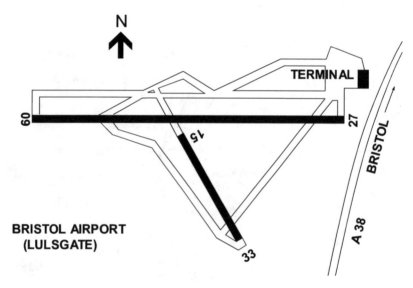

BRISTOL AIRPORT (LULSGATE)

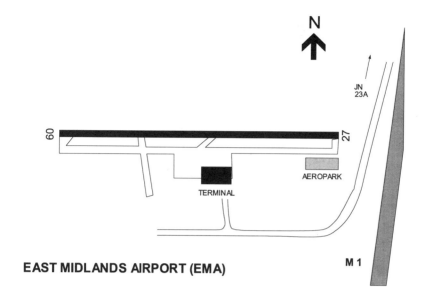

EAST MIDLANDS AIRPORT (EMA)

East Midlands International

A lovely modern terminal, being used more and more by Midlanders.
Getting there: Right alongside the M1 at junction 23A, between Loughborough and Nottingham.

Facilities: Restaurants, bars and shops. Also look out for the Aeropark, an area at the eastern end of the runway, with static aircraft displays, children's playground and a shop for aviation buffs. At the time of writing, admission to the Aeropark is £2 per car.

Flights: Lots of scheduled and charter destinations
.

Edinburgh (Turnhouse)

A good option if you live north of the border and don't fancy a day-long car ride down to Manchester.

Getting there: West of Edinburgh, signposted from the A8.

Facilities: Plenty of places to eat, drink, lounge around and shop.

Flights: Destinations aplenty on both the scheduled and charter fronts.

London Gatwick

The number one UK airport for charter flights. The airport has the older South Terminal, with the Satellite Terminal connected by monorail, and the newer North Terminal. Always bustling with holidaymakers (especially the South Terminal) and an airport with a definite feel of excitement. It tends to be a wee

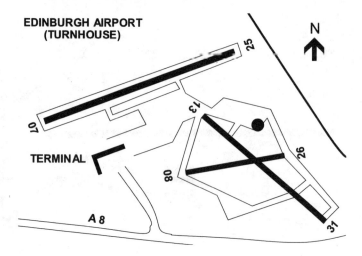

EDINBURGH AIRPORT
(TURNHOUSE)

bit prone to delays, with all that traffic trying to use a single runway, but just being there is like part of the holiday!

Getting there: South of London on the A23. Also signposted from the M23 and the M25 (London Orbital). By rail, the Gatwick Express leaves frequently from Victoria station. Coaches leave regularly from Victoria coach station.

Facilities: You name it — they've got it!

Flights: More scheduled and charter flights than you can poke a stick at. It would be easier to name the destinations you can't get to.

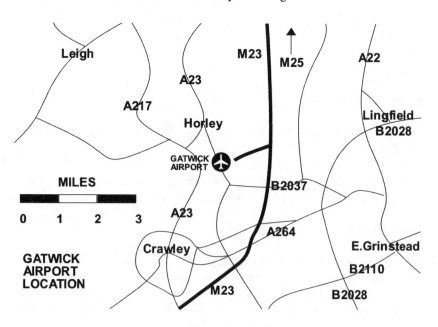

GATWICK
AIRPORT
LOCATION

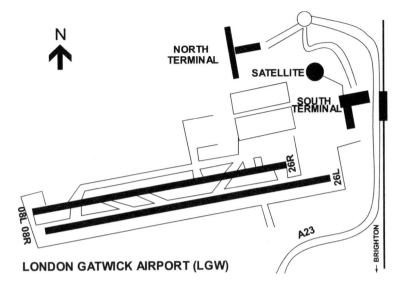

N

LONDON GATWICK AIRPORT (LGW)

Glasgow (Abbotsinch)

Getting there: West of Glasgow, signposted from the M8 at Junction 28.

Facilities: Excellent catering, bars and shops selling a wide range of goods.

Flights: Lots of scheduled services, including some intercontinental routes using wide-bodied jets. Many destinations available via charter flights.

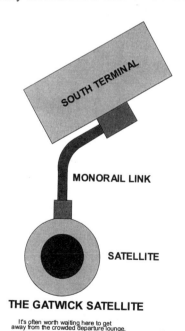

THE GATWICK SATELLITE

It's often worth waiting here to get away from the crowded departure lounge.

FLYING TONIGHT: Major UK Airports

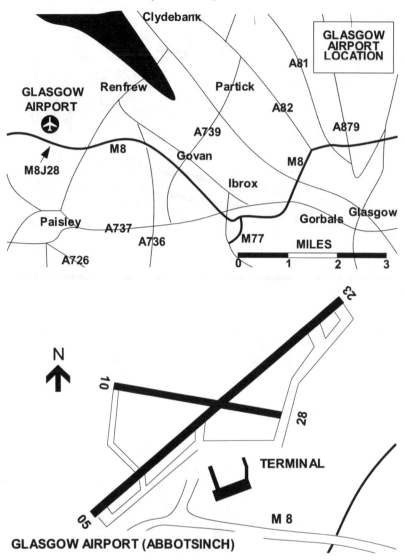

GLASGOW AIRPORT (ABBOTSINCH)

London Heathrow

What can I say ? More like a city in itself than an airport, with four terminals and all the infrastructure needed to handle 45 million passengers annually. Heathrow is one of the world's leading international airports. The statistics on Heathrow are truly staggering. Every hour, the duty-free shops sell 300 bottles of whisky, 20 bottles of champagne and 200 bottles of perfume. A total of 60 million bags are handled by the airport every year. The number of flights is now around 400,000 per annum — that's over 1,000 take-offs or landings a

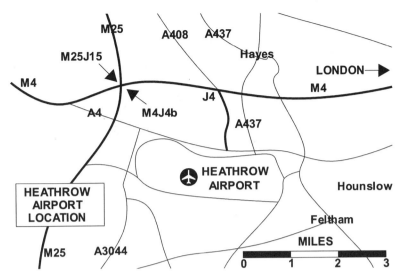

day! The airport itself contains over 40 miles of road, 15 miles of taxiway and some 6 miles of runway.

Getting there: West of London and reached easily from either the M4 or the M25. It can be reached by tube from London, using the Piccadilly Line. Make sure that you choose the right stop for the terminal you need. You can also get a coach from Victoria coach station.

Facilities: All four terminals have everything you could possibly want, although there are fewer facilities in Terminal 4 before going through Passport Control etc. Getting between terminals is easy by regular free bus service.

Flights: Virtually all scheduled services. Over 70 airlines fly into and out of Heathrow to destinations worldwide. All British Airways' intercontinental routes, together with some of its European routes and services by KLM, NLM and Air Malta, now operate from Terminal 4.

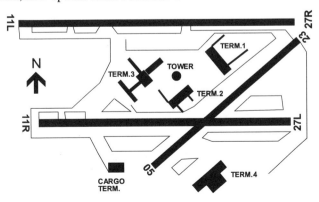

LONDON HEATHROW AIRPORT (LHR)

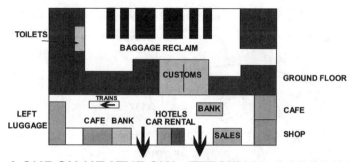

LONDON HEATHROW - TERMINAL 4 ARRIVALS
Ground Floor

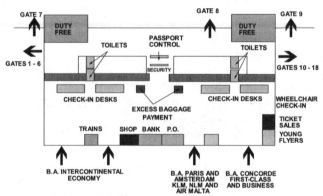

LONDON HEATHROW - TERMINAL 4 DEPARTURES

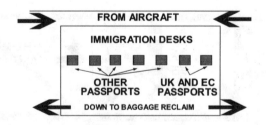

LONDON HEATHROW - TERMINAL 4 ARRIVALS
First Floor

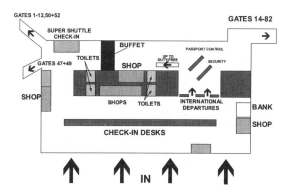

LONDON HEATHROW - TERMINAL 1 DEPARTURES

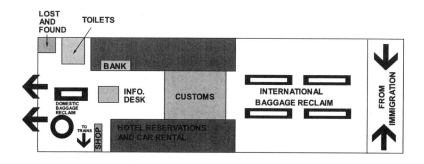

LONDON HEATHROW - TERMINAL 1 ARRIVALS
Ground Floor

LONDON HEATHROW - TERMINAL 1 ARRIVALS
First Floor

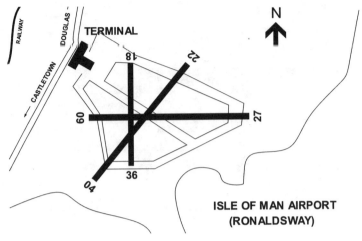

ISLE OF MAN AIRPORT
(RONALDSWAY)

Isle of Man (Ronaldsway)

Not really a major airport at all, but included because you have little choice if you live there, and a well-used holiday destination.

Getting there: Southwest of Douglas on the Douglas-Castletown road. Also connected by bus to the major Manx towns.

Facilities: Buffet, bar and restaurant.

Flights: Scheduled flights to the Mainland and Ireland etc. and the occasional charter flight.

Leeds/Bradford

Carrying less than one-tenth of the number of passengers of Manchester on the other side of the Pennines, Leeds still has a lot of potential. It is increasing in business use, particularly as a result of the success of nearby Harrogate as a

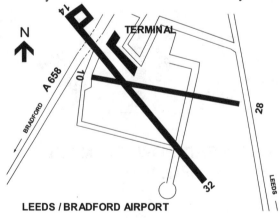

LEEDS / BRADFORD AIRPORT

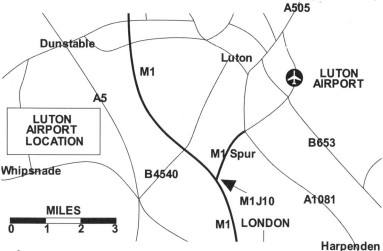

conference centre.

Getting there: North of Leeds and Bradford on the A658.

Facilities: Restaurant, bar and lounge area.

Flights: Some scheduled services and a good range of charter flights.

Luton

This is as far north as most Londoners get! Luton Airport has become a household name in the Capital as the start of a holiday.

Getting there: South of Luton and signposted from the M1 at Junction 10. Regular train services from London King's Cross/St Pancras.

Facilities: The main international terminal features restaurants, bars and shop. Also included is a 'Little Chef' restaurant. The smaller domestic terminal contains a buffet and bar.

Flights: Mainly charter flights, to a wide range of holiday destinations.

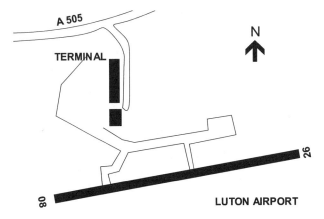

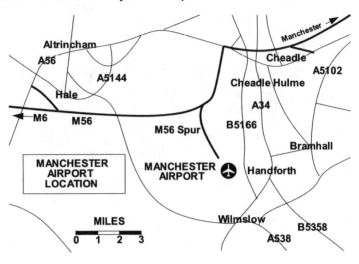

Manchester (Ringway)

Manchester is the largest airport outside London, handling over ten million passengers annually. It caters for everything from holiday charters and shuttles to wide-bodied jets serving long-haul intercontinental routes.

Getting there: South of Manchester, signposted from the M56 at Junction 5.

Facilities: The large new terminal contains a good selection of restaurants, bars and shops.

Flights: The best selection north of Heathrow for both scheduled services and charter flights. Over 40 scheduled airlines and around 30 charter operators regularly use Manchester.

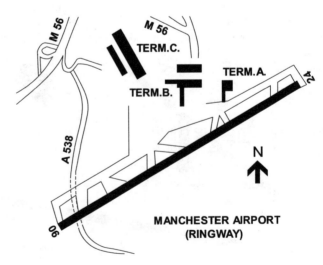

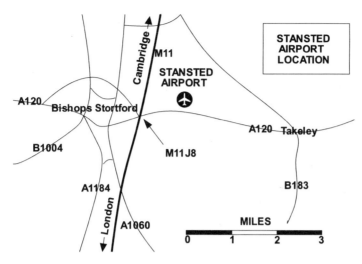

Stansted

Stansted is in the middle of an expansion phase as it takes on its new role as London's third airport. Already important as a charter flight airport, activity at Stansted is sure to increase dramatically in the next few years.

Getting there: Northeast of London, signposted from the M11 at Junction 8. Regular trains from Liverpool St station.

Facilities: The usual mix of restaurants, shops and bars.

Flights: A limited itinerary of scheduled flights, but a good selection of charter operators.

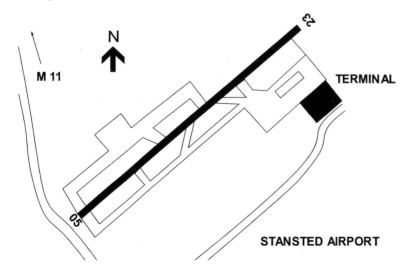

Airport Codes

All airports have identification codes which will appear on your ticket, your boarding card and your luggage tag. It's always a good idea to know the code of your destination airport, so that you can check for mistakes. Here are some of the codes of the more common destinations:

Europe

Amsterdam — AMS, Athens — ATH, Berlin — BER, Brussels — BRU, Copenhagen — CPH, Dublin — DUB, Frankfurt — FRA, Lisbon — LIS, London Heathrow — LHR, London Gatwick — LGW, Madrid — MAD, Moscow — MOW, Oslo — OSL, Paris (Charles de Gaulle) — CDG, Rome — ROM, Vienna — VIE, Zurich — ZRH

The Middle East

Amman — AMM, Baghdad — BGW, Bahrain — BAH, Beirut — BEY, Dubai — DXB, Jeddah — JED, Kuwait — KWI, Riyadh — RUH, Tehran — THR, Tel Aviv — TLV

The Far East and Australasia

Auckland — AKL, Bangkok — BKK, Beijing — PEK, Bombay — BOM, Calcutta — CCU, Delhi — DEL, Dhaka — DAC, Hong Kong — HKG, Jakarta — JKT, Karachi — KHI, Kuala Lumpur — KUL, Manila — MNL, Melbourne — MEL, Seoul — SEL, Singapore — SIN, Sydney — SYD, Taipei — TPE, Tokyo — TYO

North America

Atlanta — ATL, Boston — BOS, Chicago — CHI, Dallas — DFW, Houston — HOU, Los Angeles — LAX, Mexico City — MEX, Miami — MIA, Minneapolis — MSP, Montreal — YUL, New York (John F. Kennedy)— JFK, San Francisco — SFO, Toronto — YYZ, Vancouver — YVR, Washington — WAS

South America and The Caribbean

Bogota — BOG, Buenos Aires — BUE, Caracas — CCS, Kingston — KIN, Lima — LIM, Montevideo — MVD, Rio de Janeiro — RIO, Sao Paulo — SAO

Africa

Accra — ACC, Algiers — ALG, Cairo — CAI, Cape Town — CPT, Dakar — DKR, Dar es Salaam — DAR, Entebbe — EBB, Freetown — FNA, Harare — HRE, Johannesburg — JNB, Khartoum — KRT, Lagos — LOS, Lusaka — LUN, Nairobi — NBO, Tunis — TUN

Major Airline Codes and Contacts

NAME (CODE)	RESERVATION TEL.(UK)	NAME (CODE)	RESERVATION TEL.(UK)
Aer Lingus (EI)	081 899 4747	Emirates (EK)	071 930 3711
Aeroflot (SU)	071 355 2233	Ethiopian Airlines (ET)	071 491 9119
Aerolineas		Finnair (AY)	071 408 1222
Argentinas (AR)	071 494 1001	GB Airways (GT)	081 897 4000
Air Algerie (AH)	071 487 5903	Garuda Indonesia (GA)	071 486 3011
Air Canada (AC)	0800 181313	Gulf Air (GF)	071 408 1717
Air France (AF)	081 742 6600	Iberia (IB)	071 437 5622
Air Gambia (IV)	0293 507333	Japan Airlines (JL)	071 408 1000
Air India (AI)	071 491 7979	Jersey European (JY)	0345 676676
Air Lanka (UL)	071 439 0291	KLM (KL)	081 750 9000
Air Malta (KM)	081 745 3177	Korean Air (KE)	071 930 6513/5
Air Namibia (SW)	0293 568686	Kuwait Airways (KU)	071 935 8795
Air New Zealand (NZ)	081 741 2299	LAB Airlines (LB)	071 930 1442
Air UK (UK)	0345 666777	Loganair (LC)	041 889 3181
Air Zaire (QC)	071 434 1151	LOT Polish	
Air Zimbabwe (UM)	071 499 8947	Airlines (LO)	071 580 5037
Alitalia (AZ)	071 602 7111	Lufthansa (LH)	071 408 0442
All Nippon		Maersk Air (DM)	071 333 0066
Airways (NH)	071 355 1155	MALEV	
American Airlines (AA)	0345 789789	Hungarian (MA)	071 439 0577
Ansett Airlines (AN)	0345 747767	Malaysia Airlines (MH)	081 862 0800
Australian Airlines (TN)	081 897 4400	Northwest	
Austrian Airlines (OS)	071 439 0741	Airlines (NW)	0345 747800
British Airways (BA)	081 897 4000	Olympic Airways (OA)	081 846 9080
British Midland (BD)	071 589 5599	PIA (PK)	071 734 5544
Brymon European		Philippine Airlines (PR)	071 836 5508
Airways (BC)	0345 555800	Qantas (QF)	0345 747767
BWIA		Royal Air Maroc (AT)	071 439 4361
International (BW)	071 839 9333	Royal Brunei	
Canadian Airlines		Airlines (BI)	071 584 6660
Intl (CP)	081 667 0666	Royal Jordanian (RJ)	071 734 2557
Cathay Pacific (CX)	071 930 7878	Ryanair (FR)	071 794 0544
Cayman Airways (KX)	071 581 9960	Sabena (SN)	081 780 1444
China Airlines (CI)	071 434 0707	Saudia (SV)	081 995 7777
Continental		Singapore Airlines (SQ)	081 747 0007
Airlines (CO)	0800 776464	South African	
Cyprus Airways (CY)	071 388 5411	Airways (SA)	071 734 9841
Dan-Air (DX)	0345 100200	Swissair (SR)	071 439 4144
Delta Airlines (DL)	0800 414767	Thai Airways Intl (TG)	071 499 9113
Egyptair (MB)	071 734 2395/6	THY Turkish	
El Al (LY)	071 437 9255	Airlines (ZH)	071 499 9240

NAME (CODE)	RESERVATION TEL.(UK)	NAME (CODE)	RESERVATION TEL.(UK)
Transavia Airlines (HV)	0293 538181	Venezuelan	
Tunis Air (TU)	071 734 7644/5	Intl Airways (VA)	071 493 7287
TWA (TW)	071 439 0707	Virgin Atlantic (VS)	0293 562000
US Air (US)	0800 777333	Zambia Airways (QZ)	071 491 0650
United (UA)	0800 888555		
Varig Brazilian Airlines (RG)	071 629 5824		

Note: All telephone codes starting 0 will start 01 from April 1995.

Aircraft Registration Codes

The following is a list of the more common registration codes, identifying the country of registration of each aircraft.

Australia (VH), Austria (OE), Belgium (OO), Brazil (PP/PT), Bulgaria (TU), Canada (C), China (B), Cyprus (5B), Denmark (OY), Egypt (SU), Eire (EI/EJ), France (F), Germany (D), Greece (SX), Hong Kong (VR-H), India (VT), Italy (I), Japan (JA), Malaysia (9M), Malta (9H), The Netherlands (PH), Saudi Arabia (HZ), Spain (EC), Switzerland (HB), Turkey (TC), United Kingdom (G), USA (N).